MW01141198

Luther Burbank

To **William Crawford**

AND HIS FELLOWS OF THE

LUTHER BURBANK SOCIETY

WHOSE HELPFUL SUGGESTIONS
CORDIAL INTEREST AND
GENEROUS SUPPORT ARE
GRATEFULLY ACKNOWLEDGED

I DEDICATE THIS FIRST
PUBLISHED RECORD OF
MY LIFE WORK

Luther Burbank

LUTHER BURBANK'S EXPERIMENT FARMS SANTA ROSA CALIFORNIA

TIFFANY & CO.

Luther Burbank at Sixty-four

*This direct color snapshot of Mr. Burbank was
made on his sixty-fourth birthday, March 7th, 1913. In
California, by an act of legislature, Mr. Burbank's birthday is a state
holiday, called "Burbank Day"—taking the place of Arbor Day
in other states. On Mr. Burbank's birthday the school
children of the State plant trees and celebrate
the occasion with appropriate exercises.*

LUTHER BURBANK

HIS METHODS AND DISCOVERIES AND THEIR PRACTICAL APPLICATION

PREPARED FROM
HIS ORIGINAL FIELD NOTES
COVERING MORE THAN 100,000 EXPERIMENTS
MADE DURING FORTY YEARS DEVOTED
TO PLANT IMPROVEMENT

WITH THE ASSISTANCE OF

The Luther Burbank Society

AND ITS
ENTIRE MEMBERSHIP

UNDER THE EDITORIAL DIRECTION OF

John Whitson and Robert John

AND

Henry Smith Williams, M. D., LL. D.

VOLUME I

ILLUSTRATED WITH
105 DIRECT COLOR PHOTOGRAPH PRINTS PRODUCED BY A
NEW PROCESS DEVISED AND PERFECTED FOR
USE IN THESE VOLUMES

NEW YORK AND LONDON
LUTHER BURBANK PRESS
MCMXIV

Volume I — By Chapters

FOREWORD

Just as a stranger, going into a home for the first time, will see, vividly, either beauties or incongruities which constant association has dimmed in the eyes of the steady occupants, just so, a fresh mind may be better able to visualize the more common processes, all too familiar to me, which I employ in my daily work.

There are, in fact, many details in my routine which are no less important because they are common to me and which may need some little explanation when described to others in different walks of life.

I have, therefore, asked my associates, whose new viewpoint should enable them to observe these details in clear perspective, to present in this—the first volume, a survey of the working methods employed; so that the reader may in the first few chapters be brought to the point where he and I may go out into the fields together, and work among our plants with perfect understanding.

LUTHER BURBANK.

Santa Rosa, California
January 7, 1914.

Armored Against Its Enemies

*The desert cactus shown in the accompanying direct color
photograph print portrays a typical arrangement of armor,
although many forms of cactus are more heavily spined even than
this. In addition to the large bristling spines which fan out in
every direction, there are hidden behind each rosette a
bundle of undeveloped spines, numbering often as
high as ten thousand to each eye. When the
outward spines are cut off, these push
their way forward with surprising rapidity to protect the
gap in the armor.*

How the Cactus Got Its Spines —And How It Lost Them

A Sidelight on
The Importance of Environment

IT IS the acre-and-a-quarter patch of spineless cactus on Luther Burbank's experiment farm which first strikes the visitor's eye. In the same yard there are 2500 other experiments under way—new flowers, fruits, vegetables, trees and plants of all descriptions such as man has never before seen, but the velvet slabbed cactus—freed from its thorns—seems more than a plant transformation, it seems a miracle. Since the spineless cactus represents the typical Burbank boldness of· conception, and reflects the typical Burbank skillful execution, we may as well begin with it.

It occurred to Luther Burbank one day that every plant growing on the desert was either bitter, or poisonous, or spiny. It was this simple observation which gave him the idea of this new

[VOLUME I—CHAPTER I]

plant—a plant which already has shown its ability to outdo alfalfa five to one, and which promises to support our cattle on what have been the waste places of the world; so that our ranges may be turned into gardens to produce the vegetable sustenance for a multiplying population.

Let us look at the life story of the cactus as it unfolded itself to Luther Burbank when he realized the importance of the simple fact that desert plants are usually bitter, poisonous, or spiny.

"Here are plants," thought he, "which have the hardiness to live, and to thrive, and to perpetuate themselves, under conditions in which other plants would die in a day or a month.

"Here are plants which, although there may be not a drop of rain for a year, two years, or even ten, still contrive to get enough moisture out of the deep soil and out of the air, to build up a structure which, by weight, is ninety-two per cent. water—plants which contrive to absorb from the scorching desert, and to protect from the withering sun, enough moisture to make them nearly as juicy as watermelons.

"Here are plants which are veritable wells of water, growing in a land where there are no springs, or brooks—nor even clouds to encourage the hope of a cooling rain; here are plants which

[8]

Every Inch Protected

*Not only in the form of cactus shown here, but in
practically every form, the spines are so arranged as to protect
every inch of the surface. It will be seen that it would scarcely be
possible to touch a finger to the skin of the cactus plant above,
so completely does the armor protect it. This form of
cactus also gives an interesting illustration of the
fact that away back in its history, the plant,
instead of having flat slabs, had round
stalks. In this picture the three
joints of the round stalk
can be clearly seen.*

are rich in nutriment for man and for beast, here in the desert where the demand for food is the most acute—and the supply of it the most scanty.

"And here they are, ruined for every useful purpose, by the bitterness which makes them inedible, or the poison which sickens or kills, or the spiny armor which places their store of nutriment and moisture beyond reach.

"There must be some reason for that bitterness, that poison, those spines.

"What other reason could there be than that these are Nature's provisions for self defense?

"Here are the sagebrush, with a bitterness as irritant, almost, as the sting of a bee, the euphorbia as poisonous as a snake, the cactus as well armored as a porcupine—and for the same reason that bees have stings, that snakes have fangs, that porcupines have arrow-like spines—for self protection from some stronger enemy which seeks to destroy."

* * * * *

Self preservation comes before self sacrifice, apparently, in plant life just as it does in human life.

The plum trees in our orchards outdo each other in bearing fruit to please us; the geraniums in our dooryards compete to see which may give us the greatest delight.

ON ENVIRONMENT

But may it not be because, for generations, we have fostered them, and nurtured them, and cared for them?

May it not be because we have made it easy for them to live and to thrive?

May it not be because we have relieved them of the responsibility of defense and reproduction, that they have rewarded our kindly care by fruiting and blooming, not for their own selfish ends, but for us?

No man was ever kind to a cactus; no man ever cultivated the sagebrush; no man ever cherished the poisonous euphorbia.

Is it, then, to be wondered at that the primal instinct of self preservation has prevailed—that what might have been a food plant equal to the plum transformed itself into a wild porcupine among plants?

That what might have been as useful to the horse as hay changed its nature and became bitter, woody, inedible?

That what might have been a welcome friend to the weary desert traveler grew up, instead, into a poisonous enemy?

* * * * *

"If the bitterness, the poison and the spines are means of self defense," thought Mr. Burbank, "then they must be means which have been

[11]

acquired. The plants were here before there were animals to feed on or destroy them, so there must have been a time in their history when they had no need for such defense.

"It must be true, then, that away back in their ancestry there were desert sagebrushes which were not bitter, desert euphorbias which were not poisonous, and desert cactus plants which had not even the suspicion of a spine. It could only be the long continued danger of destruction which could have produced so radical a means of defense.

"We have, then, but to take these plants back to a period in their history before defense had become a problem—in order to produce an edible sagebrush, a non-poisonous euphorbia, a spineless cactus."

How, in a dozen years, Mr. Burbank carried the cactus back ages in its ancestry, how he proved beyond question by planting a thousand cactus seeds that the spiny cactus descended from a smooth slabbed line of forefathers — how he brought forth a new race without the suspicion of a spine, and with a velvet skin, and how he so re-established these old characteristics that the result was fixed and permanent — all of these things will be explained in due course where the discoveries involved and the working methc '

A Relic of Past Ages

The color photograph print shown above is a six time enlargement of a cactus seedling just after it has poked its head above ground. It will be noticed that the root has already shown its tendency to go deep in the ground and that this, together with the spine-covered upright stalk or slab, reflects the characteristics of immediate ancestry. The more interesting fact, however, and the fact which proved to Mr. Burbank's mind his theory of the original spinelessness of cactus, is to be found in the two smooth leaves extending from the base of the small thorny slab. These leaves, though rudimentary, and dropping off a few days after the cactus is above the ground, are reminders of a former age when all cactus plants had stalks or leaves that were as smooth as these.

employed may be made applicable, as well, to the improvement of other plants.

It suffices, here, to say that, beginning with his simple observation and reading the history of the cactus from its present-day appearance, he was able to see outlined before him the method by which a plant yielding rich food and forage has been produced, which, more than any other plant, promises to solve the present-day problem of higher living costs.

* * * * *

"But, Mr. Burbank," asked a visitor at the Santa Rosa Experiment Farm, "do you mean that the cactus foresaw the coming of an enemy which was to destroy it? Is it believable that a plant, like a nation expecting war, could armor itself in advance of the necessity? And if the cactus did not know that an enemy was later to destroy it, would it not have been destroyed by the enemy before it had the opportunity of preparing a means of defense?"

· Let us look into the history of the plant as it revealed itself to Mr. Burbank and see the answer to these questions.

* * * *

The likelihood is that parts of Nevada, Arizona, Utah and Northern Mexico were once a great inland sea—that the deserts now there were the bed of that sea before it began its long process of leakage or evaporation.

In these regions, so far as is known, the North American cactus seems to have originated.

Back in the ages before the evaporation of the inland sea was complete, the heat and the moisture and the chemical constituents of the sandy soil combined to give many plants an opportunity to thrive. Among these was the cactus, which was an entirely different plant in appearance from the cactus of today, no doubt, with well defined stalks and a multitude of leaves, each as broad as a man's head.

As the heat, which had lifted away the inland sea, began to parch its bottom, the cactus, with the same tendency that is shown by every other plant and every other living thing, began to adapt itself to the changing conditions.

It gradually dropped its leaves in order to prevent too rapid transpiration of the precious life-supporting moisture. It sent its roots deeper and deeper into the damp sub-stratum which the sun had not yet reached. It thickened its stalks into broad slabs. It lowered its main source of life and sustenance far beneath the surface of the ground and found it possible, thus, to persist and to prosper.

Perhaps there were, in the making of the

In the days when a
round stalk, and before
the animals had begun
their work of devastation,
the plant had leaves as
other plants. That this is
so is evidenced by the fact
that cactus slabs even now
put forth these leaves in
rudimentary form, the evidence of an old instinct
which has not been entirely
obliterated. Shortly after
the tiny leaves come out,
as shown in this color
photograph print, they fall
away to be followed by
the spines which push out
behind them. The likeli-
hood is that the original
leaves of the cactus
were as large as
a man's head.

desert, other plants not so adaptable as the cactus, plants which perished and of which man has no knowledge or record.

And so, we may assume, the cactus and those other plants which adapted themselves to the new conditions crowded out those which were unable to fit themselves to survive, and covered the drying plains with their verdure.

But there came animals to the bed of this one-time sea, attracted, perhaps, by the cactus and its contemporaries, which offered them food of satisfying flavor and easy access.

Of the plants which had survived the evaporation of the sea and the heat of the broiling sun, there were many, quite likely, which failed to survive the new danger—the onslaught of the animals.

Species by species the vegetation of the desert was thinned out by the elements and by the animals; and the animals, with plant life to feed on, multiplied themselves in ever increasing hordes, till perhaps the cactus was but one of a dozen plants to survive.

Then came the fight of the cactus to outdo the beasts which sought to devour it—the fight as a family, and the fight within the family to see which of its individuals should be found fit to persist.

Of a million cactus plants eaten to the ground

by ravenously hungry antelopes, we will say—
antelopes which had increased in numbers year
by year while their food supply year by year was
relentlessly dwindling — of these million plants
gnawed down to the roots, perhaps but a thousand
or two had the stamina to throw out new leaves—
and to try over again.

But just as in its previous experience, the
cactus had changed the character of its stalk, so
now it undertook another change—the acquisition
of an armor.

This armor at first consisted of nothing but a
soft protuberance, a modified fruit bud or leaf,
perhaps, ineffectual in warding off the onslaughts
of the hungry animals.

So, of the thousand or two left out of the
million, there may have been but a hundred which
were able to ward off destruction.

The hundred, stronger than the rest, though
eaten to the ground, were able still to send up new
leaves, and with each new crop the hairs became
stiffer and longer, the protuberances harder and
more pointed, until finally, if there were even only
one surviving representative of the race, there was
developed a cactus which was effectually armored
against its every animal enemy.

One such surviving cactus, as transformed
throughout ages and ages of time, meeting new

As Smooth as Velvet

A direct color photograph print of four cactus leaves after Mr. Burbank had taken the plant backward in its evolution to spinelessness. Not only have the outward spines vanished, but all of the thousands of rudimentary spines, bundled up inside, as well. Contrasted with its parent varieties, it is not only possible to handle spineless cactus with impunity, but it is so soft and velvety that it can be safely rubbed over the face. Either in the form of slabs, or cut into strips, or ground into meal, cattle instinctively prefer cactus to any other food. The elephants from a passing circus showed an immediate liking for the new food and vigorously trumpeted for more.

conditions with changes so slight as to be almost
imperceptible, but gradually accommodating itself
to the conditions under which it lived and grew—
one such survivor out of all the billions of
cactus plants that have ever grown, would have
been sufficient to have covered the deserts of the
world with its progeny—to have produced all of
the thorny cactus which we have in the world
today.

* * * * *

"You see," said Mr. Burbank, "the cactus did
not prepare in advance to meet an enemy—it
simply adapted itself to changing conditions as
those conditions arose. First, surviving the desert
drought and the broiling sun, it threw its roots
deep so that its main source of life was below
ground. Then, attacked by an enemy which ate
off the leaves above the surface, it still had life
and resistance to try again. Ineffectually, at first, it
began to build its armor, but each discouragement
proved but the incentive to another attempt. It
is a vivid picture: the whole cactus family in
a death struggle for supremacy over an enemy
which threatens its very life — millions and
millions of the family perishing in the struggle,
and perhaps but one victorious survivor left to
start a new and armored race.

"It is wonderful, too; but, whenever we plant a

cactus slab today we see evidences of adaptability more wonderful than this.

"The slab of cactus is a brilliant green as we put it in the ground. It is flat, of an oval shape, an inch or less in thickness. Its internal structure is of soft, mushy fiber, mostly water.

"As that slab sends down roots, it begins to prepare itself to bear the burden of the other slabs which are to grow above it.

"The thin, flat shape thickens out until it is almost spherical; thus presenting a curved surface in four directions instead of in two, it braces itself against the winds which will play with the new slabs far above it.

"Its mushy wood fibers grow tough and resistant; it loses much of its watery character.

"It changes in color, from green to brown; it loses its velvety skin and develops a bark like that of a tree.

"Within a year after planting, this cactus slab will have changed in appearance and in characteristics to fit itself to the new conditions which surround it.

"It will have changed its structure to bear weight and stand strains. It will have modified its internal mechanism to transmit moisture instead of to store it. It will have remodeled its outer skin to protect itself from the ground animals from

In the direct color photograph print shown here, it will be noted that the bottom slabs of the plants have lost their flat oval characteristics and have thickened out into a rounder shape, better suited to stand the strains of carrying the heavy slabs above. Also that the green color and smooth texture of the leaf has changed to woody bark, affording protection from abrasion and rodents. The transformed slab on which this plant is growing was as flat and smooth and oval and green when planted as those now above it. The photograph was made two years after planting. This is simply one of countless evidences to be found throughout plant life that plants *are what they are by reason of their environment.*

which, when it was a slab high up on another cactus plant, it knew and feared no danger!"

* * * * *

Is it more wonderful that, unseen by us, a plant should have adapted itself to the desert and, through the ages, have armored itself against an enemy, than that, before our eyes, in a single year, it should meet changed conditions in an equally effective way?

Is it more wonderful that it should grow spines than that it should grow slabs which in turn have the power to grow other slabs?

Is not the really wonderful thing the fact that it grows at all?

* * * * *

The cactus is one of the most plastic of plants— educated up to this, perhaps, by the hardships and battles through which its ancestry has fought its way.

A slip cut from a rose bush, for example, must be planted in carefully prepared ground of a suitable kind, at a certain time of the year, with regard to moisture and temperature—it must be watched and cared for until it takes root and begins for itself. Under continued cultivation, the rose bush has lost some of its ability to make its own way.

But the cactus, having come up from a line

[23]

of warriors with every hand against it, needs no such care. Every one of the fifty or more wart-like eyes on its every slab is competent to throw out a root, a fruit, or another slab—whichever the occasion seems to warrant.

Lay a cactus slab on hard ground, unscratched by a hoe, and the eyes of its under side will throw long yellow roots downward, while the eyes on the upper side await their opportunity, once the slab is rooted, to throw their other slabs and their blossoms upward.

As the tiny buds grow from the eyes, it is impossible by sight or microscopic examination to determine which will be roots, which will be fruits, or which will be other slabs. It is as though the cactus, inured by hardship and prepared for any emergency, waits until the very last possible moment to settle upon the best-suited means of reproduction—as though the bud, having started, becomes a root if it finds encouragement for roots, or a fruit if seed seems desirable, or an upward slab if this can be supported.

Nor does its attempt at reproduction require much encouragement. Fifty young cactus slabs laid on a burlap-covered wooden shelf four feet above ground were found to have thrown long roots down through the burlap and through the cracks of the boards within a few days.

[24]

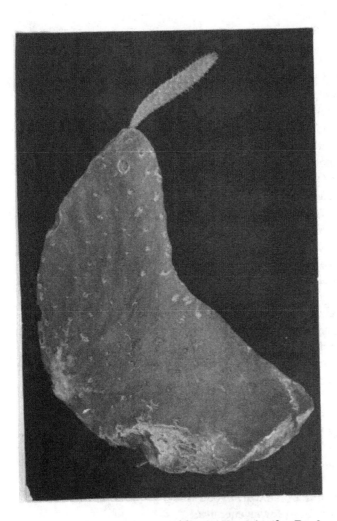

After a Year in the Dark

*The big cactus leaf shown here lay forgotten for one year, in
a dark closet in Mr. Burbank's old homestead. By accident, the
door of the closet was left open for a few days, allowed a faint light
to reach it, and the slab responded by throwing out a large but
sickly looking baby slab toward the light. During its year in
the dark, this slab of course had no moisture except what
was contained within itself and the only evidence of
its deprivation is shown by the fact that at the
bottom of the slab and in other spots the
fiber has begun to turn to wood.*

LUTHER BURBANK

A cactus plant pulled from the ground and tied by a string to the branch of a tree remained hanging in the air for six years and eight months. During this time it had no source of nourishment, and its slabs withered and turned brown. But, planted again by sticking one of its slabs six inches in the ground, it immediately took root, and within a few weeks began to throw out new blossoms and slabs.

Another detached cactus slab, long forgotten in a closet, and after having been in the dark for more than a year, was found to have thrown out a sickly looking baby slab when the closet door was left open for a few days.

The more the adaptability of the present-day cactus and its tenacious hold on life are observed, the easier it becomes to understand its fight against a devouring enemy which lived during the desert-forming age, and to see the origin of the thorny cactus of today.

*   *   *   *   *

Nor is the cactus the only desert plant which shows evidences of such a struggle.

The goldenrods of the desert are more bitte. than the goldenrods of the plains.

The wormwood of the desert is more bitter even than the wormwood which grows where there have been fewer enemies.

A Typical Cactus Flower

*However much the cactus offends by the
ugliness of its grim armor, it more than makes up by
the beauty of its flower. Most cactus flowers are large, delicate and
of brilliant color; ranging from perfect whites to deep
reds—from bright yellows to rich purples.*

The yuccas, the aloes, the euphorbias, all have counterparts in their families which, needing less protection, show less bitterness, less poison, fewer spines.

And even rare cactus plants from protected localities, and those of the less edible varieties, give evidence, by the fewness of their spines, that their family struggle has been less intense than the struggle of the cactus which found itself stranded in the bed of a former inland sea.

＊　＊　＊　＊　＊

Plants which have shown even greater adaptive powers than the cactus are to be found in the well known algae family.

One branch of this family furnishes an apt illustration of the scant nourishment to which a plant may adapt itself.

Microscopic in size, it lives its life on the upper crust of the Arctic snow storing up enough energy in the summer, when the sun's rays liquefy a thin film of water on the icy surface, to sustain life in a dormant stage during the northern winter's six months of night.

With nothing but the moisture yielded from the snow, and what nutriment it can gather from the air, this plant, called the red snow plant, multiplies and prospers to the extent that it covers whole hillsides of snow like a blanket—covers

[28]

them so completely that the reddish color of the plant, imparted to the snow, first gave rise to the tales of far northern travelers as to the color of the snowfall and explained the apparent phenomenon of red snow.

Another division of this family, going to the opposite extreme, thrives in the waters of Arrowhead Sulphur Springs in California—lives its life and reproduces itself in water so hot that eggs may be easily cooked in it.

Contrasted with these microscopic members, one thriving on the Arctic snows, the other in water at the boiling point, there is still another member of this family which has become the largest plant in the world. This, the gigantic seaweed of the Sargasso Sea, is taller and larger than the greatest giant redwood which California has produced.

And so on; some of this family of the algae grow on and in animals, some on other plants, some on iron, some on dry rocks, some in fresh water, and some in the salt seas.

* * * * *

The monkey-puzzle tree, a form of which is illustrated by a direct color photograph print, shows an adaptability to environment as striking as that of the cactus—although for an entirely different purpose.

At the top of the monkey-puzzle tree, so called,

The Monkey-Puzzle Tree

*A striking example of spines for protection, this tree
bears but few seeds and protects them, with a spiny armor,
from destruction by monkeys. The nuts are borne at, or very near
the top, and the spines are so sharp that it is impossible for
any animal to climb the tree. Where the cactus
spines are designed to protect the plant itself,
the monkey-puzzle spines are designed to
protect the offspring of the plant,
represented by its seed.*

are borne several nuts containing the seed of the plant.

In the case of the cactus the thorns were thrown out to protect the plant itself from destruction, but in the case of the monkey-puzzle tree the animals threatened not the tree itself but its offspring—its nuts were so highly prized by the monkeys, and their number was so few, that it was forced to take protective measures to keep its seed out of the reach of enemies.

From this we begin to see that each plant has its own family individuality, its own family personality. Some plants, in order to insure reproduction, produce hundreds or thousands of seeds, relying on the fact that in an over-supply a few will likely be saved and germinated; while other plants producing only a few seeds protect them with hard shells or bitter coverings, or, as in the case of the monkey-puzzle tree, with sharp spines which make access impossible.

* * * * *

In the deep canyons of California's mountains there grows a member of the lily family, the trillium.

At the bottom of these canyons there are places where the sunshine strikes but one side. The flowers on the shady side of the canyons are larger, and the leaves of the plants are broader, and the bulbs are nearer the surface than those of the plants which grow where the sun gets at them.

On the other side of the same canyons the bulbs grow deep in the soil, and the leaves and the blossoms transform themselves to protect their moisture from the sun.

Which is all that the cactus did when the sea was turned into a desert.

* * * * *

Along the Pacific coast from Or— on well down into California, there grows a con.   ɔ wild flower of the pipewort family.

Inland a little way, say ten or fifteen miles, the stalk of this plant is smooth and with hardly the suspicion of a hair. But along the shore, where the northwest winds pick up all of the finer particles from the beach and form a sand blast, the plant has developed a stalk so covered with hairs that it is as woolly, almost, as a sheep— perfectly protected against the sand-enemy.

Which is all that the cactus did when the antelopes came to destroy it.

* * * * *

Let the cactus, battle-scarred and inured to hardship, teach us our first great lesson in plant improvement:

That our plants are what they are because of environment; that simply by observing their

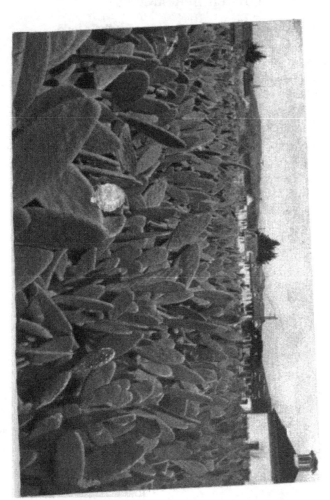

Spineless Cactus in the Patch

This direct color photograph print will give a good idea of the density which a field of Mr. Burbank's cactus attains. All of the cactus shown here is under four years old, some of it less than three. Each plant was started simply by planting a single slab in the hard adobe soil—a soil on which few useful plants will grow. On the picture which this picture was taken there is still a growth of cactus, in spite of all that has been cut off, weighing more than one million pounds. The rapidity of cactus growth is illustrated by the fact that a single hot day in June will add a ton in weight to this acre cactus patch.

structures, their tendencies, their habits, their individual peculiarities, we can read their histories
back ages and ages before there were men and
animals—read it, almost, as an open book; that
our plants have lived their lives not by quiet
rote and rule, but in a turmoil of emergency;
and, just as they have always changed with their
surroundings, so now, day by day, they continue
to change to fit themselves to new environments;
and that we, to bring forth new characteristics in
them, to transform them to meet our ideals, have
but to surround them with new environments—not
at haphazard, but along the lines of our definite
desires.

*—Is not the really
wonderful t h i n g
the fact that the
plants grow at all?*

Twenty-Three Potato Seeds
AND
What They Taught

A Glimpse at
the Influence of Heredity

THE springtime buds unfold into leaves
before our eyes—without our seeing them
unfold. We have grown accustomed to
look for bare limbs in March; to find them hidden
by heavy foliage in May; and because the process
is slow and tedious, and because it goes on always,
everywhere about us, we are apt to count it
commonplace.

Just as we can understand that the tree in our
yard, responding to its environment—to the April
showers, to the warm noons of May, to the heat
of summer and to the final chill of fall—has
completed a transformation in a year, so, too,
can we more easily understand the gradual transformation of the cactus in an age. So, too, can
we realize that the individual steps between the
first ineffectual hairy protuberance, and the final

spiny armor, each a stronger attempt to respond to environment, were so gradual as to be almost imperceptible.

* * * * *

But those rudimentary, half formed leaves which come forth from every eye of the cactus slab before the thorns or fruits come out—those leaves which, as if seeing that they have no useful purpose, as if realizing that they are relics, only, of a bygone day, drop off and die—what environment has acted to bring them forth?

And those two smooth slabs that push out when the tiny seedling has just poked its thorny head above the ground—to what environment do they respond?

How shall we account for this tendency in a plant to jump out of its own surroundings, and out of the surroundings of its parents, and their parents and those before them—and to respond to the influences which surrounded an extinct ancestor—to hark back to the days when the desert was the moist bottom of an evaporating sea and before the animals came to destroy?

* * * * *

A group of scientists were chatting with Luther Burbank when a chance remark on heredity led one of them to tell this bear story.

It seemed, so the story ran, that a baby bear

had been picked up by miners within a few days after its birth—before its eyes had opened. The cub, in fact, was so small that it was carried several miles to the camp tied in the sleeve of the coat of one of the miners.

Raised to adult bearhood by these miners, without ever having seen another bear—relieved of the necessity of finding its own food and removed from the wild environment of its ancestors—this bear became as thoroughly domesticated, almost, as a tabby cat.

What would such a bear do if thrown on its own resources? Would it have to begin at the beginning to learn bear-lore?

Bears are great salmon fishers, for example.

But is this skill taught by the mother to the baby bear—or is it a part of every bear at birth? That was the question of interest.

When the animal had arrived at maturity, it was taken, one day, to a shallow salmon stream.

Here was a bear which had never fished for salmon, and had never tasted fish; a bear which, if bears have a language, had not received a moment of instruction in self support; a bear which, taken before its eyes were open, had never seen its mother, had never known an influence outside of the artificial atmosphere of the mining camp.

Brought to the salmon stream, however, there was not an instant of delay; it glanced about, located a natural point of vantage, straddled the brook with its face down-stream, and bending over, with upraised right paw, waited for the salmon to come.

It did, unhesitatingly, just what any normal wild-raised bear would have done.

With wonderful dexterity it was able to scoop the onrushing salmon out of the stream and to throw them in an even pile on the bank with a single motion.

As other bears would do, this domesticated bruin stood over the stream until it had accumulated a considerable pile of the salmon on the bank.

Going to this pile it quickly sorted over the fish, making now two piles instead of one—*with all the male salmon in one pile, and all the female salmon in the other.*

Then, with its sharp claw, it proceeded to split open the female salmon and to extract the roe, which it ate with relish. This consumed, it finished its meal on the other meat of the fish.

Untaught, it recognized salmon as food; distinguished males from females; knew the roe as a delicacy. Unpracticed, it knew, instantly, just how to fish for salmon and how to find the roe.

An Ancestral Secret

When the rapid growing eucalyptus tree pushes out its leaves it discloses one of the secrets of its ancestry. Some of the leaves, like those at the top of the branch pictured above, are narrow and long. Others, lower down, are much broader. On a single tree it is common to find five or six different kinds of leaves seeming, when laid side by side, as though they must have come from separate plants. The history of the eucalyptus, as disclosed by its leaves, its quick growth, and other characteristics, is that one time it was an herb —perhaps an annual. To fit themselves to some new environment, its ancestors succeeded in establishing themselves as perennials. But this change was so recent that the evidences of the transition are still to be found in the leaves of all young eucalyptus trees today.

"Right here on this experiment farm," spoke up Mr. Burbank, "you might find hundreds of evidences of heredity more striking than that— more striking because they are the evidences of heredity in plant life, instead of in animal life.

"Right here," said he, "you will find plants which show tendencies unquestionably inherited from a line of ancestry going back perhaps ten thousand years or more—tendencies, some of them, which now seem strangely out of place because the conditions which gave rise to them in their ancestors no longer exist; tendencies like those of the cactus and the blackberry to protect themselves from wild beasts when wild beasts are no longer enemies; tendencies to deck themselves in colors designed to attract the insects of a forgotten age—insects which, perhaps, no man has ever seen.

"Where some incredulity might be expressed as to whether the bear had not actually been taught to fish for salmon, or seen another bear perform the act, there can be no such question in the case of heredity in plants.

"Here," said he, as a bed of sweet peas was approached, "is a plant which has inherited the climbing, twining tendency.

"That is an evidence that, at some time back in its history, this plant has probably been crowded for room. Plants which grow high do so usually because, at some stage in their existence, they have had to grow high to get the sun and the air which they need. Low-lying plants, like the pumpkin for example, give evidence that they have always enjoyed plenty of space in which to spread out.

"The bear of your story may have slipped away, unknown to its keepers, and seen another bear fish for salmon; but if these tendencies and traits, and if the ability to perform the feats necessary for existence are not passed down from mother to son—if they do not come down through the line of ancestry, if all of the old environments of the past have not accumulated into transmissible heredity, what enables that sweet pea to twine around the stake?"

* * * * *

"A closer observation of the· sweet pea will show us that its tendrils are really modified leaves, produced, like the spines of the cactus, by ages of environment which, added up, combine to make heredity; and that their actual sensitiveness to touch is so highly developed that they almost instantly encircle and hold fast to any suitable support within their reach.

"It would be interesting to take a motion picture of a sweet pea as it grows, as similar

[41]

Unblended Heredities

*The two dahlias shown in this direct color photograph
print illustrate the freaks which heredity sometimes plays.
Sometimes, when two widely separated strains of heredity are brought
together in a single plant, or animal, the result is a blend; but
in these dahlias, as will be seen, some of the petals take
back to one line of ancestry while others take back,
equally distinctly, to another. No man can
predict the outcome when two separate
strains of heredity are mixed.*

motion pictures have been taken; making our separate snapshots one every three minutes instead of fifteen or sixteen to the second, so that the reel would cover a period of fifteen days; then, with a fifteen day history recorded on our film, to run it through the projecting lantern at the rate of fifteen or sixteen pictures to the second, thus showing in seven or eight minutes the motions of growth which actually took fifteen days to accomplish; on the screen before us, with quick, darting motions, we should see the sweet pea wriggle and writhe and squirm—we should see it wave its tendrils around in the air, feeling out every inch within its reach for possible supports on which to twine.

"We should see, by condensing half a month of its life into an eight minute reel, that this sweet pea has inherited an actual intelligence—slow in its operation, but positive, certain—an inherited intelligence which would be surprising, even, in an animal."

*　　*　　*　　*　　*

"All through plant life we find these undeniable evidences of heredity.

"I have here, for example, two tiny seedlings which look almost alike. They are distantly related. One is the acacia and the other the sensitive plant.

The tiny seedlings shown here are the sensitive plant and its unsensitive cousin, the acacia tree. Although these plants are clearly related, and resemble each other as seedlings, one has the sensitive, shrinking tendency, while the other, through its lack of it, testifies to an entirely different heredity.

In this print it is seen that the sensitive plant, at the left, folds its leaves into the smallest possible compass, making itself as inconspicuous as possible to an approaching enemy. The actual photograph was snapped less than two seconds after the plant had been touched—but in that brief time, as is shown, the transformation was complete. The one at the right, with its different heredity, shows no tendency to fold up, even when crumpled in the hand.

"Much as these plants look alike, they bear witness to the fact that they have within them two entirely different strains of heredity.

"The acacia will permit us to touch it and handle it without showing signs of disturbance.

"But its cousin, in the same soil, and of the same size, immediately folds up its leaves, in self protection, at the slightest touch.

"From this we read the fact that one branch of this family has found it necessary to perfect a form of self defense, while the other has had no such experience in its life history."

*   *   *   *   *

"I have been much interested lately in an experiment with common clover—in producing clover leaves with wonderful markings.

"The only way in which I can account for the markings with which some clover leaves will bedeck themselves is that, in the heredity of the plant, there was a time when, not being poisonous itself, it tried to simulate the appearance of some poisonous plant, to protect itself from insects.

"At first thought, it might require a stretch of the imagination to understand how this could be—yet a closer inquiry shows that the process was as gradual and as surely progressive as the transformation of the cactus.

"In clover, as in other plants, there has always

Simulating a Poisonous Look

*The clover leaves shown above reveal a strange inherited
tendency. It is Mr. Burbank's belief that the white markings
and the black splotches, which can be readily distinguished, represent
an attempt on the part of the plant to simulate a poisonous look,
as a means of self protection. Although the tendency to
protect themselves with these warning streaks and
blotches of color is very strong, yet in all of
his experiments, Mr. Burbank has not
found a single clover plant which
was actually poisonous.*

been variation—some few individual clover plants have always had the white and black markings.

"At some time in the history of the plant those without the markings have been destroyed, and so, responding to this new environment, the markings became more and more pronounced until now we have not only white triangular markings, but ugly black splotches going clear through the leaf.

"From these markings we can read the history of the clover—most of the family having plain leaves inherited from an ancestry which found no need to protect itself from an enemy—with an occasional outcropping of poisonous-looking color splotches—the inheritance of scattering environments in which self protection was necessary."

*   *   *   *   *

"Or we might consider the ice-plant, so called, which protects itself from the heat of the sun by surrounding itself with tiny water drops which have the appearance and serve the same purpose as icicles; or the wild lettuce, known sometimes as the compass plant, which turns its leaves north and south so that only their edges are reached by the sun; or any of a number of other strange protective measures which plants have perfected— all manifestations which would be impossible if heredity were not an ever present, controlling influence.

[48]

A Living Refrigerator

*In this direct color photograph print it will be seen that
the stems and leaves are covered with formations which appear
to be tiny icicles. The plant is known as the ice plant, and the
icicles, in fact, are stored up moisture which it saves up against
the heat of the sun. The need for this extra moisture
is not apparent where this plant now grows, and
it is reasoned, therefore, that the plant
has been stranded, at some time or
another in its history, in some
unusually hot, dry climate.*

"We have, too, in many parts of the country plants which have learned to snare and trap insects and even animals, and to digest them and to live on them.

"Among these carnivorous plants are the common pitcher plants, and the Venus fly trap.

"The pitcher plants, instead of belonging only to one family, are to be found in a number of different families, thus showing that environment has produced a similar strain of heredity in separate kinds of plants which are not kin to each other.

"One of the pitcher plants which grows abundantly in the moist places of the Sierras and in northern California even catches frogs, small animals and birds. The plant seems especially devised to lure the animals into its pitcher. Above the pitcher is a little lattice and an opening, like a window, through which the light can shine. The insects and the animals see a haven from the sun and rain, and as they go in, there are little fingers on the plant which push them along and keep them from coming back.

"Once securely in the trap, the plant secretes a digestive juice, like our own gastric juice, and absorbs the animal life as food.

"In these traps it is common to find all kinds of insects—including the undigested wings and

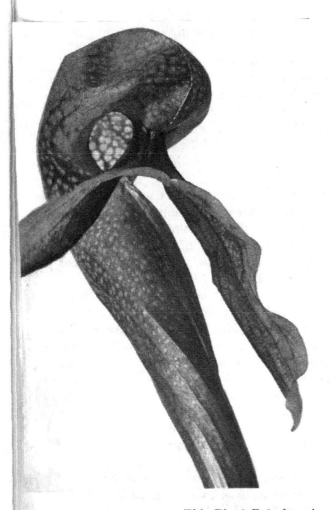

This Plant Eats Insects

The pitcher plant, shown here, which grows in the high mountains of California, has perfected an ingenious contrivance for catching and digesting insects. At the top of the pitcher, so called, seen above, there is an opaque lattice work in the interstices of which is a translucent, mica-like substance. The insect, entering from beneath, in search of shelter, finds itself in a cosy chamber, well lined, and weather proof. Once inside the chamber, however, it discovers that it is being swallowed, irresistibly—and the plant finally deposits it in the stomach below, where it digests it with a secretion akin to hydrochloric acid. There are several other known carnivorous plants, showing that at some time in their ancestry, the soil has not given them sufficient nutriment for their needs.

legs of beetles and grasshoppers and the bones of toads and frogs.

"Is this not a more wonderful manifestation of old environment, recorded within a plant in the form of heredity, than even that of a bear which seemed to have inherited the intelligence and skill to fish?"

*　　*　　*　　*　　*

"To my mind," said one of the scientists, "the by-product of your work is fully as interesting as the work itself—the viewpoint which you get on the forces which control life is of even greater attraction to me than the wonderful productions which you have coaxed from the soil."

"A by-product, no," said Mr. Burbank; "these things are a vital part of the day's work. Heredity is more a factor in plant improvement than hoes or rakes; a knowledge of the battle of the tendencies within a plant is the very basis of all plant improvement. It is not, as you seem to think, that the work of plant improvement brings with it, incidentally, a knowledge of those forces. It is the knowledge of those forces, rather, which makes plant improvement possible."

*　　*　　*　　*　　*

"There are really, after all, only two main influences which enter into the make-up of life— only two influences which we need to direct, in

[52]

order to change and control the characteristics of any individual growing thing.

"The first of these is environment.

"The rains, the snows, the fogs, the droughts—the heat, the cold—the winds, the change in temperature between night and day—the soil, the location in shade or sun—competition for food, light, air—the neighbors, whether they be plant neighbors, or animal neighbors, or human neighbors—all of these, and a thousand other factors which could be thought of, are the elements of environment—some pulling the plant one way and some another, but each with its definite, though sometimes hardly noticeable, influence on the individual plant.

"And the second is heredity:

"*Which is the sum of all of the environments of a complex ancestry—back to the beginning.*"

*   *   *   *   *

"Just as with the bear, if the story be true, so in plant life. In every seed that is produced there are stored away the tendencies of centuries and centuries of ancestry. The seed is but a bundle of tendencies.

"When these tendencies have been nicely balanced by a long continuation of unchanging environment, the offspring is likely to resemble the parent.

[53]

"But when, through a change of environment, that balance is disturbed, no man can predict the outcome.

"So when a seed is planted, no man can be sure whether the twentieth century tendencies will predominate; or whether long-forgotten tendencies may suddenly spring into prominence and carry the plant back to a bygone age."

*   *   *   *   *

"How can seeds store up the tendencies of their ancestry?" some one asked Mr. Burbank.

"How can your mind store up the impressions which it receives?" he asked in reply.

*   *   *   *   *

Hidden away in the twists and turns of our own brains, needing but the right conditions to call them forth with vividness, there are hundreds of thousands, perhaps millions of impressions which have been registered there day by day.

The first childhood's scare on learning of the presence of burglars in the house may make us supersensitive to night noises in middle age.

The indelible recollection of a mother's love and tenderness may arise, after forty years, to choke down some harsh word which we are about to utter.

The combined impressions of a thousand experiences with other human beings seem to blend together to help us form our judgment of a single human being with whom we are about to deal.

As the weeks have rolled into months, and as the months have melted into years, new impressions have arisen to crowd out the old; stronger impressions have supplanted the weak, bigger impressions have taken the place of lesser ones—but the old impressions are always there—always blending themselves into our judgments, our ambitions, our desires, our ideals—always ready and waiting, apparently, to single themselves out and appear before us brilliantly whenever the proper combination of conditions arises.

So, too, with the seed.

Every drought that has caused hardship to its ancestors is recorded as a tendency in that seed.

Every favoring condition which has brought a forbear to greater productiveness is there as a tendency in that seed.

Every frost, every rain, every rise of the morning sun has left its imprint in the line of ancestry and helped to mold tendencies to be passed from plant to plant.

Beneath the wooden looking, hard sheathed covering of the seed, there is confined a bundle of tendencies—an infinite bundle—and nothing more.

One tendency stronger than another perhaps—a good tendency suppressing a bad tendency—or the other way; tendencies inherited from immediate parents, tendencies coming down from wild ancestry, tendencies originating from the influences of twenty centuries or more ago—tendencies which are latent, awaiting only the right combination of conditions to bring them to life; all of the tendencies of a complex ancestry—some lulled to sleep, but none obliterated; that is a seed.

*　*　*　*　*

"The whole life history of a plant," said Mr. Burbank, "is stored away in its seeds.

"If we plant enough of the seeds, in enough different environments, we are sure to have that life history with all of its variations, all of its hardships, all of its improvements and retrogressions, uncovered before us."

*　*　*　*　*

Which brings us to the boyhood lesson which Luther Burbank learned.

*　*　*　*　*

Thomas A. Edison spilled chemicals on the floor of a baggage car—lost his job as train boy—and made electricity his vocation instead of his avocation.

Luther Burbank found a seed ball on one of the plants of his mother's potato patch.

Who knows what little thing will change a career? Or what accident will transform an ideal.

[56]

Typical Potato Seed Balls

*The print above shows potato seed balls such as Luther
Burbank, in his boyhood, found. The potato has become so
accustomed to being reproduced by the division of its tuber that seed
balls are now a rarity. And, while the tuber produces
potatoes true to type, the seed balls, the rarer they
become, seem to lose all connection with the present,
and grow into potatoes which hark back to the
long-forgotten traits of old heredity.*

Or what triviality, out of the ordinary, will lead
to the discovery of a new truth?

*   *   *   *   *

The potato seed ball was a little thing, an
accident almost, a triviality, at least, so any practical farmer would have said.

Away back in the history of the potato, when
it had to depend upon its seed for reproduction,
every healthy potato plant bore one or more.

But years of cultivation have removed from
the potato the necessity of bearing seeds for
the preservation of its race. The potato plant, so
certain, now, to reproduce itself through subdi-
vision of its bulb or tuber—so reliant on man for
its propagation—has little use for the seed upon
which its ancestors depended for perpetuation
before men relieved it of this burden.

So the average potato grower, knowing that
next year's crop depends only on this year's
tubers—and being more anxious, alas, to keep his
crop at a fixed standard than to improve it—might
see the occasional seed ball without knowing its
meaning—or realizing its possibilities.

Luther Burbank saw the seed ball in his
mother's potato patch. If he did not realize its
possibilities, at least he scented an adventure.

And who can say in advance where adventure
—any adventure—will lead?

ON HEREDITY

How Mr. Burbank lost the precious potato seed ball, how he found it again, and then nearly spoiled the outcome by not knowing how to plant the seed—and the practical lessons in method which he learned—these are things which will be explained at length in the proper place.

The interesting fact to be noted here, however, is that, from this seed ball, he produced twenty-three new potato plants.

Each of these plants yielded its own interesting individual variations—its own interpretation of long-forgotten heredity.

One, a beautiful, long potato, decayed almost as soon as dug; another was red-skinned with white eyes; several had eyes so deep that they were unfit for use; all varied widely.

The twenty-three, in fact, represented as many different stages in the history of the potato family; and, having no present-day environment to hold them in balance, all were unlike any potato which had ever been cultivated.

Among the number, though, was one tuber better than the rest—and better than any potato which Luther Burbank had ever seen. That tuber was the parent of the almost universally grown Burbank potato of today.

When Luther Burbank selected from his twenty-three potato seedlings what eventually was

Some Potato Seedlings

A direct color photograph print of different kinds of potatoes produced from a single potato seed ball. It will be seen that while all of these potatoes are small, some are more shapely than others and at the bottom of the picture will be seen a common variation of tubers known as "snake potatoes." These forms represent different stages in the history of the potato and almost any potato seed ball will give variations as wide or wider than these.

to become the parent of a new race of potatoes, it may be said that he was then fairly started on his successful career of plant improvement.

Had he rested on his honors and been satisfied with this single new production, the world would always have been his debtor.

For up to that time the potatoes of the world were small, more or less uncertain of bearing, and of mediocre yield. The older varieties—disregarding the fact that their yield was but one-fourth of the present production, would find no buyers in our markets.

With the same work—indeed with less—both the pioneer who grew potatoes for his own sustenance and the potato specialist who produced his crop on a commercial basis, were able to quadruple their output—to make four measures of food—four measures of profit—grow where but one had grown before.

And today, when more pounds of potatoes are grown than of any other food crop of the world, the increase made in a single year's crop—the increase gained without any corresponding increase in capital invested or cost of production—amounts to an astounding sum in the millions.

Possibly at no other time in the history of the nation could the Burbank potato have c...me more opportunely.

These were the days when Chicago was a far western city, and when the great territory beyond was the home of the pioneer.

The potato is a vegetable designed peculiarly for the pioneer.

It requires no great preparation either for planting or harvesting. It grows rapidly on the rich new soil turned over by the settler; a little cultivation insures its growth; when ripened it may lie in the ground and be used as needed; when the fall frosts come it can easily be banked in a pit for winter use.

Little care; small outlay; easy preparation for food; these make the potato the first crop to be grown when the settler locates his new home.

Trace now the influence which this one success had upon a growing nation. It was in 1871. It was a time when the line between success and failure—between starvation and comfortable plenty—was drawn so finely for the pioneer that even the slightest help was of a value out of proportion to its intrinsic worth.

A crop failure or shortage, in those reconstruction days after the war, meant a set-back that would take years to overcome, for the pioneer's only source of supply, usually, was his own crop.

Any increase, therefore, in Nature's products— such as the potato—in the days of the pioneer,

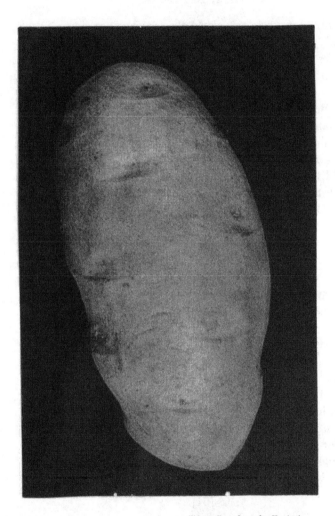

The Burbank Potato

An improvement in one of the most important crops which, as has been stated by a member of the United States Department of Agriculture, is adding seventeen million dollars a year to the farm incomes of America alone, to say nothing of foreign countries. This potato was produced by Mr. Burbank when in his 'teens, and was the result of finding a seed ball on his mother's potato patch. The perfection of this potato involved no form of crossing or hybridization, but was brought about solely through utilizing the forces of environment and heredity— and by careful selection.

signified more to the world than it ever has since. Multiplying a potato yield by four, then, meant more than were such a yield multiplied by ten, or even by a hundred, now.

* * * * *

But the greatest value which the Burbank potato gave to the world was not in the increase in its potato crop; the greatest service it rendered was not even the seventeen-million-dollar-a-year addition to America's farm incomes which this potato has been estimated to have wrought.

The greatest value it gave—the greatest service it performed—was to turn Luther Burbank into a new line of invention—into a line in which, because it is so basic and so vast, even a slight improvement means a fortune to the world of consumers—and the perfection of a new food or forage plant untold billions in added wealth.

* * * * *

It was the potato seed ball, found by Luther Burbank, the boy, which gave the world Luther Burbank, the man.

It was his success with the potato which put in his heart the courage to forswear the certainty of farming for the ups and downs of an inventor's life; and it was the lesson in heredity which it taught that placed him on the trail of Great Achievement.

[64]

ON HEREDITY

Plant potato eyes, and you get potatoes like the parents—improving, or retrograding, a little, according to the present environment in which they grow.

But plant potato seeds, and you tap a mine of heredity, infinite in its uncertainty, but infinite, too, in its possibility.

That was the boyhood lesson which Luther Burbank learned.

We shall see, now, how he applied it to other plants—how he built on it and expanded it—and how it became the basis of more than 100,000 later experiments in plant life.

—Heredity is the sum of all of the environments of a complex ancestry back to the beginning.

Some Dooryard Geraniums

*The geraniums pictured here are such as
might be found in any American dooryard. And,
because they are common, we are too apt to lose sight of the
wonderfully ingenious system, described in this chapter,
which has been built up to insure variation.*

No Two Living Things
Exactly Alike

Infinite Ingenuity
the Price of Variation

W HERE do the flowers get their colors?"
asked a visitor of Mr. Burbank one
day.

"From the bees, and the butterflies, and the
birds," was the reply. "And from us."

* * * * *

Let us pick up a geranium, such as might be
found in any dooryard in America, and see what
Mr. Burbank meant.

If we were to strip off its five brilliant petals
soon after they have opened, and slice the base of
the blossom in half, we should find ourselves
looking into a tiny nest of geranium eggs—round,
white, moist, mushy eggs with a soft skinny
covering for shells.

Carefully packed in a pulpy formation, these
eggs, we should observe, are incased in a well
protected nest, longer than its breadth, oval, except

[VOLUME I—CHAPTER III]

that its top extends upward in the form of a single
tiny stalk.

Surrounding this neatly packed nest of geranium eggs with its single upright stalk, and
hugging it closely all around, we should see ten
modified leaves, a quarter of an inch or so in
length, ending, each, in a pointed stalk as big
around, perhaps, as a bristle out of a hair brush;
ten such leaves in two rows—as if shielding the
egg chamber and its central stalk from harmful
intruders.

At the tops of the ten surrounding stalks, we
should see the crosswise bundles, nicely balanced,
of beautiful golden-orange pollen dust, loosely
held in half-burst packages.

And at their base, we should find the syrup
factory of the geranium—a group of tiny glands
which manufacture a sticky confection that covers
the bottom of the flower with its sweetness.

Shall we take one of the egg-like seeds from its
nest and plant it? We might as well plant a
toothpick.

Shall we take a package of the pollen, and
put it in the ground? We might as well sow a
thimbleful of flour.

But let us combine one of those eggs with a
grain of that pollen, and three days in the soil will
show us that we have produced a living, growing

thing—a new geranium plant, with an individuality, a personality, of its own—an infant geranium, which we for the first time have brought into being —a thing which has never lived before, yet which has within it all of the tendencies inherited from ages of ancestry—tendencies good and tendencies bad, which wait only on environment to determine which shall predominate.

By the simple combination of the pollen and the egg we have produced an entirely new plant, which may, if we will it, become the founder of a whole race of new and better geraniums.

*   *   *   *   *

How shall we go about it to make a combination, such as this, between the pollen dust and the seed-like egg so snugly stowed away within its nest?

Let us examine that central stalk inside the double guard of pollen-bearing stamens and we shall have the answer.

As the stamens fall away we begin to see a transformation in the stalk. Its upper end, which at first seemed single, now shows a tendency to divide into five curling tendrils—moist and sticky.

Though we may plant pollen in the ground without result, we have but to place it on one of these sticky tendrils as they curl from the end of that central pistil stalk to start an immediate and rapid growth.

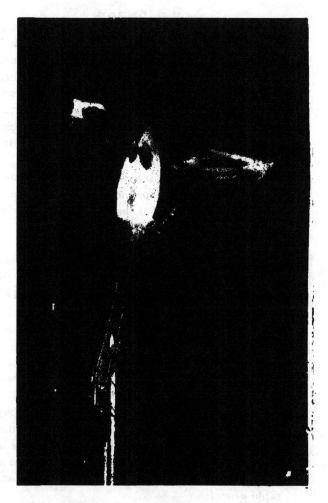

The Geranium Ready to Give Pollen

This direct color photograph print shows the stamens of a geranium, greatly enlarged, as they cluster around the pistil at the time their pollen is ready for the entering insect. Each of the five stamens bears an anther, or pollen sac, which, as will be seen, bursts open and turns inside out when the pollen is ready.

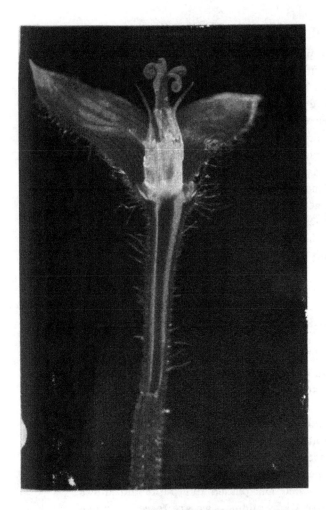

The Geranium Ready to Receive Pollen

*As soon as the pollen has been removed from the geranium,
its stamens shrink and wither away, disclosing the pistil which
they have surrounded. The pistil then opens up its stubby end into
five curling lobes, as seen above, upon whose sticky surface
the pollen from other flowers finds lodgment.*

Once planted there, the pollen grain begins to throw out a downward shoot, into and through the pistil stalk—forming itself into a tube which, extending and extending, finally taps the egg chamber and makes possible a union between the nucleus of that pollen grain and the egg below which awaits its coming.

So, to produce a new geranium we have but to dust the grains of pollen upon the sticky stigma of that central pistil stalk; and when the flower has withered away, its duty done, we shall find within the egg chamber a package of fertile geranium seed ready for planting.

* * * * *

But there arises, now, a difficulty. While those little packages of pollen dust are there, the central pistil stalk inside keeps shut up tight, and it has no sticky surface on which to dust the pollen.

And if we search for another blossom which shows an open, sticky pistil, we shall find that the pollen packages which once surrounded it have gone.

To make our combination between the pollen grains and the egg-like seeds, therefore, we find it necessary to search first for one blossom which is in its pollen-bearing stage, and then for another blossom which has passed this point and shows a receptive sticky stigma—we are forced to make

How the Carnation Insures Variation—I

This direct color photograph print, greatly enlarged, shows that the carnation has perfected a device for insuring variation equally ingenious as the geranium's. This photograph shows the pistil, arising from the yellowish egg nest, closed and unreceptive at the time that the pollen, which may be seen on the two stamens at its right, is ready for distribution.

How the Carnation Insures Variation—II

The pollen has now disappeared from the anthers and the pistil spreads to receive pollen from a neighboring carnation. The fuzzy, sticky surface of the receptive portion of the pistil may be seen in this photograph.

How the Carnation Insures Variation—III

*This direct color photograph print shows the housing
of the carnation's egg nest cut away, and the individual eggs
closeted beneath the pistil awaiting fertilization
can be clearly distinguished.*

the combination between the two, instead of between the pollen grains and the eggs of a single blossom.

*   *   *   *   *

Which is exactly what the Mother Geranium intended we should do.

*   *   *   *   *

If the stigma of a blossom were at its receptive stage when the pollen packages around it burst open, there would probably be combined in the seeds of its egg chamber below, only the characteristics of one parent plant—only the tendencies of a single line of ancestry.

The geraniums growing from those seeds would be so like in their tendencies of *heredity* that they would differ, individually, only as their individual *environments* differed.

But when those eggs have brought to them the pollen from another plant, there are, confined within them, the tendencies and characteristics of two complex lines of ancestry; so that the plants into which they grow will be encouraged into variation and individuality, not as a result of environment alone, but as a result of the countless tendencies inherited from two separate lines of parentage.

What a scheme for pitting the old tendencies of heredity against the new tendencies of environment—what an infinite possibility of combinations this opens up!

* * * * *

Truly of a million geranium blossoms no two *could* be exactly alike—nor any two of their five million petals—nor any two of their ten million stamens—nor any two of their hundred million honey glands—nor any two of their billion pollen granules!

* * * * *

What we have seen in the geranium—those seed-like eggs, the sticky stigma and that microscopic pollen dust, we may see in some form or other in every plant that grows.

The act which we might have performed to produce a new geranium plant—the combination of one of those seeds with some of that pollen— is going on about us always, everywhere—with the bees, and the butterflies, and the birds, and the winds, and a score of other agencies acting to effect those combinations.

Which is the reason for the candy factory at the bottom of every geranium's little central well. And for those brilliant petals, and that delicate scent, and the picket arrangement of the stamen stalks, and the crosswise poise of their pollen-bearing anthers, and the central pistil stalk which rises upward from the egg nest—and everything that is

[77]

beautiful and lovely in the bloom of that geranium
—and the geranium itself.

* * * * *

Here is a plant, the geranium, so anxious to
produce variations in its offspring that it has lost
the power of fertilizing its own eggs and risked
its whole posterity upon the coöperation of a
neighboring plant.

It has no power of locomotion—no ability to
get about from place to place in search of pollen
for its eggs or of eggs in need of its pollen; nor
has its neighbor; so they call in an outside
messenger of reproduction—the bee.

The geranium makes its honey at the bottom
of its blossom. It places movable packages of
pollen dust balanced on springy stamens in such
a way that, to reach the sweets, the pollen hedge
must be broken through. It keeps its egg chamber
closed and its pistil unreceptive while the pollen
dust is there, and as if to advertise its hidden
sweets to the nectar loving bees, it throws out
shapely petals of brilliant hue and exudes a
charming scent.

And thus, the bees, attracted from afar, crowding into the tiny wells to get their sweets, become
besmeared with pollen dust as they enter a pollen
bearing bloom—and leave a load of pollen dust
wherever they find a receptive stigma.

A Pollen Laden Bee

This direct color photograph print shows a bee, greatly enlarged, which was captured in a cactus flower. The pollen grains can be seen sticking to its hairy body, and the fact that, as it crawls into the next flower, some of this pollen will find lodgment on the sticky surface of a receptive stigma is easily realized. The bees gather pollen not only for distribution but for their own uses. The two large splotches of pollen shown beneath the second pair of legs are "pollen dough" which the bees carry home for food.

LUTHER BURBANK

Where did the geranium get its color?

"From the bees," said Mr. Burbank.

Just as the cactus covered itself with spines until it had built up an effective armor, in the same way the geranium, by easy stages, has worked out a color scheme to attract the bees upon which it depends to effect its reproduction.

*   *   *   *   *

In Mr. Burbank's yard there grows, as this is written, a Chinese arum whose color and whose scent reveal a different history.

Unlike most common flowers which advertise to bees and birds and butterflies, this plant sends its message to the flies.

Flies feed on carrion. The nectar of clover is not to their liking and the brilliant colors of our garden flowers fail to attract them. Our refuse is their food, and they are guided to it by colors and scents which are offensive to us.

So this Chinese carrion lily, as it has been named—stranded at some time in its history, perhaps, in some place where flies were its only available messengers of reproduction, or blooming at a period when other means were not within its reach—has bedecked its spathe with a rich and mottled purple—in color and in texture resembling, from a distance, the color and texture of a decaying piece of liver.

[80]

A Fly-Loving Flower

The Chinese carrion lily pictured here, advertises to the flies to act as its messengers of pollenation. The spathe frequently grows to eighteen inches in length and, as can be seen, though rich and really beautiful, is of the same color as a piece of decaying liver. The smell emitted from this flower is offensive in the extreme—all an advertisement to the flies, which are carrion-loving insects.

Just as the geranium supplements its advertisement in color with an advertisement in scent, so, too, the carrion lily has developed an individual odor-appeal, decidedly like that of meat too long exposed to the sun.

So obnoxious and so penetrating is the odor of this flower that each year it has been found necessary to cut down the plant shortly after it has bloomed.

And so truly has it achieved its ideal that even the buzzards, carrion birds that they are, attracted by its color, its texture and its smell, have descended in ever-narrowing circles—only to fly away in disgust when they found they had been lured by a flower.

* * * * *

Where the geranium finds it satisfactory merely to block the entrance to its honey store with an array of pollen bundles which must be pushed aside by the entering insect, the Chinese carrion lily makes doubly sure of pollenation by means of a still more ingenious device.

The fly, attracted by the color of the spathe and guided by the hidden odor at the base of the flower, lights on the sturdy spadix and uses it as a ladder for descent. The opening around the spadix is just large enough to afford a comfortable passage way; but once within the well, the spathe closes in and snugly hugs the spadix, so that the fly, buzzing about in the chamber below, becomes thoroughly covered with the pollen dust.

This done, the flower slowly unfolds and permits the pollen laden insect to escape.

* * * * *

Many other flowers show equal or greater ingenuity.

In some varieties of the sage, the pollen-bearing stamens actually descend and quickly rub the yellow dust on either side of the insect, after which they fall back into their former position above the nectar cells.

Most of the orchids, too, show an unusual ingenuity.

One species bears its pollen in small bundles, the base of each bundle being a sticky disc. The structural arrangement of the flower is such that the insect cannot secure its nectar without carrying away at least one of the bundles. A pollen bundle glues itself to the head of the insect and curves upward like a horn.

As soon as the insect has withdrawn from the flower, this pollen horn bends downward in front of the insect, close to its head, so that when the next flower is entered the dust can hardly fail to reach a receptive portion of the pistil.

In this orchid there is but a single receptive

[83]

The Orchid Awaiting an Insect

*Flowers are usually not only designed by their general
shape to attract insects, but their nectar store is often surrounded by a target of some kind—sometimes of color only, and
sometimes as in the case of the orchid, a folded leaf which guides the
insect in. Almost all flowers, in this way, have centers which
are white, or more brilliant than, or different from the
rest of their color, as if to lead the insect to its
work with the least possible delay. The
orchid's pollen may be seen in this
photograph print directly in the
center of the flower.*

The Orchid's Pollen Bundles

With the rest of the blossom torn away, the orchid's
pollen bundles and its sticky stigma may be seen in this
photograph print. These bundles attach themselves to the head of
the insect, sticking out like a horn so that the next flower visited will
be sure to receive its charge of pollen. The sticky stigma
can be seen in this print directly beneath the two pollen
bundles at the top. The petal itself of course
is bent down to show the structure, but it
can be seen that the colors and all
of the lines lead to the central
point as if to guide the bee.

stigma and the pollen bundles are separate and single, too; but in another orchid which has two receptive stigmas, the pollen bundles are in doublets, held together with a strap.

Thus the insect visiting this second orchid carries away two pollen bundles on its forehead, each so nicely placed that their dust will reach both sticky stigmas of the next flower entered.

* * * * *

Similarly, the pollen of the milkweed is stored in two little bags, connected by a strap. When the bee visits the flower its feet become entangled in this strap and when it leaves it carries both bags with it.

And so, throughout the whole range of plant life, each fresh investigation would show a new display of ingenuity—infinite ingenuity directed toward the single end of combining the tendencies of two lines of heredity—so that the offspring may be different from and better than the parent.

We should see that there are those flowers which bloom only in the night. Flowers which, as if having tried to perfect a lure for the insects of the day, and having failed, have reversed the order of things and send forth blossoms of white or yellow—luminous colors always—to attract the moths that fly after the sun goes down.

We should find many interesting half hours

A Humming Bird Flower

*The common nasturtium may be taken as a type of
flower which advertises to the birds rather than to the bees.
The honey is stored at the bottom of a long tube down which a
bee could hardly stretch its proboscis. In many other ways,
including the arrangement of the stamens and pistils,
bird flowers show their adaptation to the partnership which their ancestors have built up.*

of wonder contemplating such flowers as the honeysuckle, the nasturtium and many of the lilies—which have taken special precaution to place their nectar in long, horn-like tubes, out of the reach of insects, so that only the birds may become their messengers of reproduction.

We should see the pathos of those flowers which advertise for insects that rarely come. The barberry, for example, which can be pollenated only during the bright hours of a cloudless day, and during a time so short that there is little chance of pollen being brought by insects from other blossoms. Each barberry blossom, ready for the insect if it should come, but as if expecting disappointment, makes sure of self perpetuation, if not of self improvement, by jabbing its pollen laden anthers on its own stigma with a motion as positive and as accurate as the jump of a cat.

Or the fennel flower of France, in which the several pistils bend over and take pollen from the stamens around them and straighten up again.

Or the flowers of the nettle, in which the stamens increase their height with a sudden spring-like action, showering the pollen up over the receptive stigma.

We should observe that wheat and some of the other grains, as though discouraged by centuries and centuries of failure to secure variation, had settled down to the steady task of reproducing their kind exactly as it is, depending only on individual environment for individuality, and ensuring reproduction by self pollenation.

We should see plants in all stages of their attempts to keep their kind on the upward trend; we should see a range of ingenuity so great that no man, no matter how many of his days have been devoted to the study of plants and their ways, can ever become dulled to its wonders.

* * * * *

"I bought some extremely expensive seed corn several years back," complained a Santa Rosa farmer. "But, just as I expected, it ran down. The first year's corn was fine, and so was the second; but now it has gone clear back to ordinary corn. This plant improvement doesn't pay."

"Do you know how corn reproduces itself?" asked Mr. Burbank.

"Do you realize that if you plant good corn on one side of a fence, and inferior corn on the other, the corn cannot see the fence?

"Would you expect that a cross between a race horse and some family dobbin would produce a line of racers?

"Separate your good corn from your poor, and keep it by itself, and you will find that it does not run down, but even gradually improves."

LUTHER BURBANK

Every farmer knows that corn must be planted in large quantities close together—that a single kernel of corn, planted in one corner of a lot, apart from other growing corn, would be non-productive.

Yet how many of those who depend upon corn for their living fully realize the reason for this?

The geranium, with its nectar, its scent, its color and its structural arrangement, has built up a partnership with the bee to perform its pollenation.

While corn, with no advertisement, no honey, no brilliant reds, no scent, has developed an equally effective plan of making the breezes act as its messenger of reproduction.

* * * * *

Here is a plant, tall and supple, that responds with graceful movements to the slightest breath of air. At its top it holds a bunch of pollen laden tassels—swaying tassels which, with each backward and forward movement, discharge their tiny pollen grains in clouds, which slowly settle to the ground.

Below, on the stalk of the plant, are the ears of corn, containing row after row of the egg kernels, needing but combination with pollen from above to become, each, a seed capable of starting another corn plant on its life.

An Experiment in Corn

The ear of corn shown at the left is one which, on an ordinary corn plant, was allowed to take its course. The other ear is one which was covered with a paper bag at the time when the pollen was flying. The strands of silk thus being protected from pollen, the kernels beneath did not mature. It will be seen from this that the breezes are as necessary to the corn plant as the bees and birds are to the flowers.

Just as the eggs of the geranium were housed in a protective covering, so, too, the corn eggs are sheathed in protective husks. And just as a tiny stalk protruded from the egg chamber of the geranium, so, too, does the silk which protrudes from the end of the husk serve the same purpose for the corn seed.

Tear the husks from an ear of corn, and it will be seen that each strand of the protruding silk goes back to an individual kernel on the ear. That, between the rows of kernels, like electric wires in a conduit, each strand of the common bundle of silk protruding leads back to its separate starting place.

To combine the characters of two parent corn plants, all that is necessary is to dust the pollen from the tassel of one on the silken ducts of the ear of another.

And the breezes, as they swish a waving field of corn gracefully to and fro—as they play through a forest of pines, or as they ripple the grasses of our lawns—are performing their function in the scheme of reproduction as effectively as the bee does when it goes from geranium to geranium in search of sweets.

* * * * *

Consider the simple salt-water cell, as seen reproducing itself under the microscope merely by splitting in two; and those two each becoming two, and so on endlessly.

Observe that, with only a single line of parentage from which to draw tendencies, the individualities to be found in this, the lowest form of life we know, are molded wholly by the difference in the saltiness of the water, or the variation in its temperature, or those other limited changes within a short-lived environment.

And then consider the geranium, and the Chinese arum, and the orchid, and the corn—with a thousand added complications in their lives brought about by a single dominant purpose—a thousand self-imposed difficulties and obstacles which would be needless except for that guiding desire to give the offspring a better chance than the parent had!

What a price to pay for variation! What ingenuity and effort each new combination of heredities has cost! How many must have been the plants which advertised for insects that did not come! How many, finding themselves in an unequal struggle, have perished in the attempt!

* * * * *

Truly, if the cost of things may be taken as a measure of their value, how much must this dearly bought variation be worth in the Scheme of Things!

LUTHER BURBANK

"The struggle of a plant to secure variation in its offspring does not end with the seed," said Mr. Burbank. "It only begins there."

* * * * *

In the tropics, a common tree near the seashore is the coconut palm. The coconuts which we find in our market, their hard shells outermost, are but the inside portion of the nuts as they grew on these trees.

When they were gathered, there was a fibrous substance surrounding the shell an inch or two in thickness—a woody fiber torn off by the shippers to cut down the cost of freight and cartage. Around this excelsior-like covering, as the nut grew on the tree, there was a skin-tight, waterproof cover, with a smooth or even shiny surface.

At the top of the nut as it would stand if it floated in water, are three well defined eyes.

Since these coconut palms grow, usually, along the water's edge, the nuts often roll into a brook, or a river, or the ocean, and float away.

Once detached from the tree and started on such a journey, the eyes disclose their purpose. Two of them begin to throw out a system of roots, not on the outside of the coconut, but growing at first within the woody fiber between the shell and the outside skin.

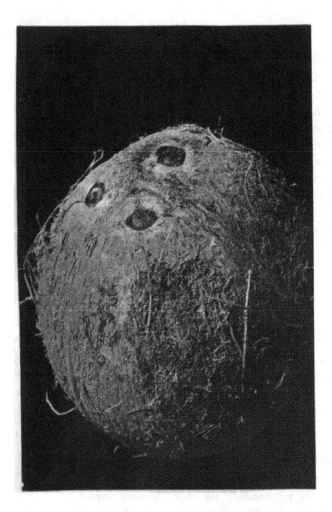

The Coconut's Three Eyes

*As this coconut falls in the water, one of the eyes shown
at the top throws up a sail-like leaf while the other two begin to
throw out a mass of roots within the excelsior-like covering, but inside
of the waterproof cover of the nut, which for the purpose of illustration, has been removed. When the sail has carried the
nut to a new environment, the roots burst forth and
the sail grows into a taller stalk, which finally
becomes the trunk of the new palm.*

At the same time the other eye pushes out sail-like leaves extending several inches above the outer casing.

Then, with sails set, and aided by the current of the stream, the nut starts out on its journey to find an environment of its own.

Once landed, after weeks, perhaps, of travel, the roots which have been growing inside force their way out into the moist soil at the water's edge—the sail leaves begin to grow into stalks, which later develop into the trunk of the tree, the waves start to build new ground by washing sand around it, and the first page in the history of a new palm in a new environment is written.

* * * * *

The hard shell surrounding the stored-up milk in the coconut is there, obviously, as a protection from the monkeys; to prevent extermination through their liking for the milk.

And that excelsior packing, and that waterproof housing, are these not as plainly the palm's attempt to provide for its baby tree a new environment?

* * * * *

We do not have to go to the tropics for evidences like these.

There is probably no more familiar weed in our vacant lots than the common dandelion.

ON VARIATION

Who can forget its feathery seed ball waiting, when ripe, for the first youngster, or the first draft of air to blow it away on its long sail through the air as it distributes its seeds—some on stones, perhaps, and some on plowed ground—such a multitude of seeds that, though many be lost, some will find themselves throwing roots into new soil, rearing their heads into new air—starting life in a new environment?

*   *   *   *   *

Or we might learn a lesson from one of the wild chicories which provides some of its seeds with wings to fly, while others it leaves wingless. Those seeds without wings fall at the feet of the parent plant as if to keep green the old family home; while those with wings fly away to start new families, under new conditions, where latent traits and tendencies—latent elements of weakness or strength—may coöperate to produce a better chicory.

Or from that joy of childhood, the squirting cucumber, which, when ripe, fires its seeds, mixed up in its milky contents, with such force that they are sometimes carried a distance of twelve to fifteen feet.

Or even the sweet pea, or our garden pea, which when their seeds have dried, have the ability to throw them some distance from the parent plant.

LUTHER BURBANK

In Mexico, there is the familiar jumping bean tree, which calls in an insect to aid in the distribution of its seeds.

While these beans are still green, they are visited by a moth which lays her eggs in them. As they ripen, the grub hatches out and lives upon the food stored within.

As if in partnership with the moth, the jumping bean tree has provided food for her offspring, so that the larva has plenty to eat without injuring the seed within the bean.

And the grub, as it hollows out the bean and jumps about within it, causes it to turn and roll— rolls it into a new environment—repays its family debt to the tree which gave it food.

* * * * *

In the wooded mountains near Santa Rosa there grows a pine tree which has worked out an ingenious scheme for taking advantage of occasional forest fires to aid it in its reproduction.

Most other trees mature their nuts or seeds and shed them every season. The animals may eat the fruit and carry the seeds afar, or take the nuts to new environments, or the seedlings may come up at the foot of the parent tree—but the process of seed bearing and seed shedding usually completes its cycle every fall.

The pine tree referred to, however, does not

shed its seeds in this way, nor is there any inducement in them or their covering to tempt an animal to carry them away.

They grow in clusters about the trunk and branches, but remain attached to the tree. The cones which hold them do not even open. Sometimes nine or ten crops of these seed cones may be observed clinging to a parent tree.

But whenever the woods are visited by a forest fire, the cones are dried out by the heat, and the seeds, released, fall to the ground and sprout.

In the localities in which these trees grow, there would be little chance for their seeds to germinate, in fact, except after a forest fire had cleared the ground.

Against the competition of all of the hardy underbrush to be found in those localities, the mother tree, it would seem, fears that her seeds will have but a poor chance.

Yet when the fires have cleared the ground and killed almost every other living thing, these seeds spring up almost as quickly and almost as thickly as grass on a lawn; and, competition removed, they grow with surprising rapidity into the making of a new forest.

It has been observed that these trees grow usually along the sides of deep canyons where the destructiveness of the fire is the greatest—and only in canyons where forest fires are frequent—showing that without the aid of the fires, the tree can not perpetuate itself.

So firmly fixed has this partnership between the fires and this particular pine tree become that its seeds, if planted under other conditions, will not germinate.

Taken from the tree, it is impossible to get them to grow even with the greatest care in good soil; but experiment has shown that, if placed for a few hours in boiling water, they will readily sprout even in poor soil.

Thus, as if through a strange alliance, the forest fires clear the ground, scatter the cones and prepare the seed of this pine tree for germination; and the pine tree, in turn, rebuilds the forest which the fires destroyed.

* * * * *

The devil's claw, a tropical relative of our unicorn plant, has developed the power to bite and to hold on with almost bulldog grip, in its scheme of providing new environments for its young.

This plant, growing low on the ground among other tropical vegetation where the distribution of seed becomes a problem, grows a seed pod of seven inches or more in length.

Its seed pod, while maturing, is encased in a

The Devil's Claw—I

*As it grows in the tropics, the seed pod of the
devil's claw, or martynia, shown above, resembles a large
gourd in color and in texture of its covering. The succeeding
prints show how it transforms itself to bite and hold
on to passing animals with a bull dog grip.*

pulpy covering with a thick green skin, and its bulb and hook suggest some kind of gourd.

When the seeds within are mature, the outside covering splits and peels away, disclosing a seed nest which is armored with spines more thickly than a prickly pear. That which, during its early stages, formed the hook, now spreads into two branches with pointed ends sharper than pins, almost as sharp as needles.

Between these four-inch hooks, where they join the spiny bulb behind them, there appears a hole from which the seeds, if loosened from their former pulpy support, may, by pounding and thumping, find their way out into the world.

As the seed pod lies on the ground, its sharp hooks coiled in exactly the right position, it awaits a passing animal. This spring trap may remain set for many months, but once an animal, big or small, steps between those fish-hook points, their mission is accomplished. The first slight kick or struggle to get away imbeds them deeply, and at each succeeding struggle the hooks bite in, and in, and in, until finally the animal, in its efforts for release, pulls the seed pod from the plant and starts to run.

Swinging to a leg or tail, suspended by the two sharp points of its prongs, the spiny housing of the seed pod comes now into play. At each bound

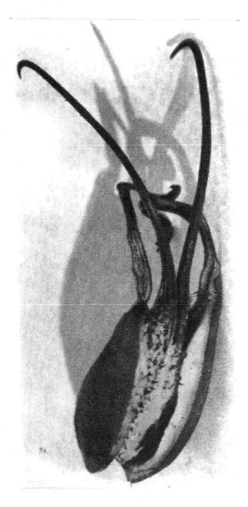

The Devil's Claw—II

In this print it will be seen that the gourd-like covering is being shed, and that what at first seemed to be but a single stem has separated into two wiry prongs. seed pod is attached to the plant by a stem which joins it at the bottom of the picture shown above.

The Devil's Claw—III

*Having completely shed its gourd-like covering, and with
its jaws set for a passing animal, it will be seen that the pod
itself is covered with prickly spines. When the fish-hook points of
the prongs bite into the leg of an animal, the whole contrivance becomes
balanced from that point, and at each jolt and jounce the heavier body
of the pod pounds down upon the leg, its spines causing great
pain. There is an opening between the two prongs at the
upper end of the pod itself from which the seeds
come out at every bounce. When these are
scattered over a mile or two of new
environment, the pod falls apart.*

or jump, the pod flops up and down, and its prickly points, adding to the pain of the ever-pinching hooks, are sure to keep the animal in motion. As the frightened beast makes haste to get away from an enemy which it cannot see, the seeds within the pod begin to loosen and fall out on the ground.

When the last seed has left its shelter, the trap begins to fall apart—its object accomplished—its seeds scattered throughout a mile or more of new environment.

*   *   *   *   *

The sailor is awed by the mountains, and the mountaineer is awed by the sea.

And we, too, are more apt to wonder at the jumping beans of Mexico and at the devil's claw of the equator than at the cherry tree in our own back yard—which outdoes both of these by forming a double partnership.

Just as the geranium bids for the bees, so the cherry blossom, with its delicate pink and its store of honey advertises for butterflies and bees to bring the pollen from a neighboring tree.

And this partnership concluded, the accounts balanced and the books closed, it then seeks new partners in the birds.

That delicious meat around the seed, that shiny skin of red, and that odor of the cherry as it ripens —these are a part of the advertisement to the

[105]

birds or animals—a lure to get them to eat the fruit and carry the seed as far as they may to another—a new—environment.

Shall we wonder at the jumping bean and the devil's claw when our own cherry tree is getting the bees to give its offspring new heredities and the birds to surround these heredities with new environments in which to grow?

*   *   *   *   *

Wherever we look we see a new display of ingenuity—all for the sake of variation—variation which may mean retrogression as well as advancement—but such infinite variation that, surely, there can be found one out of a thousand, or one out of ten thousand, or one out of a million better than those that went before.

Every flower that delights our eye, and every fruit which pleases our palate, and every plant which yields us a useful substance, is as delightful as it is, or as pleasing or as useful as it is, *simply because of the improvement which has been made possible through variation.*

—No two living things are e x a c t l y alike.

The Rivalry of Plants
to Please Us

On the Forward March
of Adaptation

W E cut down our alfalfa four or five times a season," says some one, "why doesn't it grow spines to protect itself? We destroy our lettuce before it goes to seed; why doesn't it develop a protective bitterness like the sagebrush?

"We rob our apple trees of all their fruit the moment they are ripe; why do they not become poisonous like the desert euphorbias?"

* * * * *

"Let us go back to the cactus," says Mr. Burbank, "and read the answer.

"Grim and threatening though the cactus seems, it is not without its softer side; in the springtime its blossoms, a multitude of them, push their way through the spiny armor—and rival the rose in formation, compete with the orchid in the delicacy of their hues.

[Volume I—Chapter IV]

LUTHER BURBANK

"No favorite garden flower can outdo this ungainly monster of the desert, when in bloom, in the seductiveness of its advertisement to the bee.

"When summer comes, and the bee has paid, by the service it has rendered, for the honey it has taken, the nest of fertile eggs beneath each cactus blossom begins to grow into a luscious fruit.

"In this cactus fruit there is an acid sweetness as tempting as that of the raspberry, the strawberry or the pineapple. Its outward covering has a brilliant beauty no less attractive than that of the cherry, or the grape.

"Thus, in the springtime, the cactus, like the cherry, advertises to the friendly bees to bring its offspring new heredities, and, in the fall, it advertises to the friendly birds to carry off its seed and plant it where its young may have the advantage of new environments.

"In its spiny armor we read the plant's response to the enemies in its environment.

"In its brilliant flowers and tempting fruit we read its receptiveness to the friendship of the birds and bees.

"Those spines and those flowers and fruits tell us that while its ancestors were fighting a common foe, they still found time to build up lasting partnerships.

ON ADAPTATION

"And so, with every plant that grows, we shall see these same tendencies—instincts shall we call them?—to ward off the enemy and make use of the friend."

* * * * *

"So long as plants grow wild, the frosts, the winds, the hail storms, the droughts and the animals are principal among the enemies with which they have to reckon.

"So long as they grow in the woods, or on the mountains, or in the deserts, the bees and the birds and the butterflies—the warmth of the sun and moisture of the soil—these are among the friendly factors in their lives.

"But when we take plants under cultivation, we upset their whole environment.

"We build fences around our blackberries so that they need no thorns. We save the seeds of our radishes, and the bulbs of our lilies, and through human organization distribute them and plant them wherever they will grow. We cut slips from our apple trees and ship them from county to county, and state to state, and nation to nation, and zone to zone. We select, and improve, and plow, and harrow the ground for our plants; we water them when they are dry; we surround them with shade trees if they need shade, we cut down the shade trees if they prefer the sun; we plant their baby seedlings under glass, and give them every favoring condition in which to mature; we remove what for ages have been the chief problems of their lives—we take over their two prime burdens, the burdens of self defense and reproduction.

"The frosts, and the winds, and the hail storms, and the droughts, and the animals are no longer the chief enemies of plants; for man, when he comes into their environment, is more dreadful than all of these combined—if he chooses to destroy.

"And the bees and the birds and the butterflies, and the warmth of the sun, and the moisture in the soil, fade into insignificance as friendly influences when compared with that of man—if it pleases him to be a friend.

"So the geranium still advertises to the bees, and the cherry tree to the butterflies and birds, as of old.

"But their main advertisement, now, is an advertisement to us; their strongest effort, now that we have become predominant in their lives, is to lure us with their blossoms and their fruit—to enchant us with their odors, and colors, and lusciousness, as they formerly enchanted only the bees—to win and hold our appreciation and affection, and merit our kindly attention and care."

ON ADAPTATION

Our alfalfa, lettuce and apples, like our horses, our cows, our dogs, have found in man a friend stronger than the strongest of their enemies.

So their welfare now is measured by the usefulness of the service they can render in repayment for man's care.

*　*　*　*　*

"There is a common snowball in my yard," continued Mr. Burbank, "which advertises alone to me.

"In the woods around there are other snowballs of the same family—wild snowballs—into whose life history man, as a part of environment, has never come.

"The wild snowball, with only a fringe of blossoms, and a mass of egg nests and pollen inside the fringe, is still advertising to the bee.

"But the snowball in my yard has responded to my care, and to the care of those who went before me, till its stamens and pistils, as if seeing their needlessness, have turned to blossoms—till its eggs have grown sterile, even should an insect come.

"And so, with every snowball which grows in anybody's yard—cultivation has relieved it of the need for reproduction, and what was once but a fringe of flowers has been transformed into a solid mass of blossoms.

The Snowball, Tame and Wild

*The upper snowball is the one which grew in Mr.
Burbank's yard, or such as commonly grows under cultivation.
The snowball below is a wild one such as grows in the woods. The
wild snowball, it will be seen, uses the flowers to attract
messengers of pollenation to the reproductive mechanism
which the flowers encircle. The upper snowball,
however, has lost its power of reproduction by seed and advertises to us,
instead, to perpetuate its race.*

ON ADAPTATION

"Just as a mother cat can make a dumb appeal
for the protection or the sustenance of her kittens,
an appeal no human being can misunderstand,
just as strongly and just as clearly do the
snowballs, by the beauty and helplessness of their
self-sterilized flowers, appeal to us to see to their
protection and effect the perpetuation of their
kind."

     *   *   *   *   *

Many violets, as they grow wild in the woods,
bear two kinds of blossoms.

One is the flower, rich in color and in scent,
which is borne at the top of the plant.

The other, an egg nest without odor, or beauty,
or other advertisement—which is borne near the
base of the plant.

The flower at the top, like the flower of a
geranium, advertises to the insects to bring pollen
from other plants.

The colorless flower at the bottom needs no
insect to bring it pollen—it pollenates itself and
produces fertile eggs with only a single strain of
heredity.

Some of these violets with upper and lower
blossoms, particularly those which grow in the
shade, never open their upper flowers—as if
knowing that the friendly insects so prefer the sun
that no attempt at advertisement could lure them

[113]

to the shade. These violets reproduce themselves wholly by the self-fertilization which goes on within the colorless flower below.

And there are those violets, of this same kind, blooming in the sunlight, which open their upper flowers, so that, if visited by insects, the seed within matures; but, as if in doubt of the effectiveness of their advertisement, the lower blossoms continue to produce their inbred seed.

And there are still other violets which, as if assured of the friendship of the insects, have ceased to make the colorless blossoms below, and produce their entire output of seed at the base of the brilliant upper flower.

Here, in these three kinds of violets, is written the story of a plant's struggle with wild environment in which man has not yet become a factor; the story of an unequal struggle in which the stages of failure, partial victory, and complete triumph are clearly laid before us.

*   *   *   *   *

Into the life of the violet, some few hundred years ago, there came the new element of environment—man.

A single violet plant which was taken from its catch-as-catch-can existence, let us say, found itself in fine-combed soil in the shade of some on·' dooryard.

At the base of this plant, in the center, may be distinguished the colorless flowers of the violet which need no insect to bring them pollen, but which, fertilizing themselves, reproduce offspring with but a single strain of heredity.

If it rained too much, drainage took up the excess. When the rains did not come, the soil was sprinkled.

Under cultivation, and kindly care, the discouragements of its life grew less and less, and the encouragements to thrive grew more and more.

Soon this violet, as if assured of reproduction, abandoned the blossoms at its base, and threw its energies into making bigger and brighter and more beautiful blossoms at its top. Where it had half-heartedly advertised to the bees of old, it now concentrated its efforts to win the approval of the new-found friend whose dooryard brought it opportunity.

And this is the life story of that kind of violet which we now call the pansy.

On the one hand, in the woods, we see its wild kin-folk still struggling against unequal odds; on the other we see its own large, beautiful pansy petals, and the increased brilliancy of its hues; each a response to environment.

Truly, in the pretty face of the pansy, we may read the vivid story of man's importance as a friendly element in the lives of plants.

*　*　*　*　*

Where do the flowers get their colors?

"From the bees," said Mr. Burbank. *"And from us."*

The Violet's Wonderful Advertisement

*With both wondrous color and charming scent, some
violets advertise to the insects which, because of the flower's
preference for moist shady places, rarely come. Wild, in the woods, are
to be found violets which bear only colorless flowers as shown
in the preceding print, as well as some which bear both
kinds of flowers, and still others which, as if having
succeeded in attracting the insects, bear
only the delicate blossoms shown here.*

A Response to Kindly Care

*Taken from its wild environment and freed from its
struggle, the violet became a pansy. Truly, in the pretty face of
the pansy, we may read the vivid story of man's importance as a friendly element in the lives of plants.*

ON ADAPTATION

On the experiment farm at Santa Rosa, there grow two ordinary looking pear trees which amplify the thought.

One of these trees produces large, juicy, soft, aromatic, luscious, easily digested pears—a delight to the eye and to the palate.

The other produces small, hard, bitter, indigestible fruit, the very opposite in every way of our idea of what a pear should be.

Looking at these trees side by side, it would be difficult to realize that their fruit could be so different. Both show the unmistakable characteristics of the pear tree—the pear tree shape, the pear tree branches, the pear tree leaves, the pear tree blossoms. In their fruit alone do they differ.

* * * * *

Since these two pear trees illustrate an important point, let us begin at the beginning:

The pear, it seems, was first discovered in eastern Europe or western Asia. It was there, in Eurasia, some two thousand years ago, that man first realized that this fruit was good to eat.

Coming to us, thus, out of obscurity, the pear, during these twenty centuries, has spread to the east, and to the west, till it has completely encircled the globe—a slow process, but one which takes place in every desirable fruit which is discovered or produced.

LUTHER BURBANK

As Europe became more and more settled, the pear kept pace with the invaders. It followed them to the British Isles, it followed them across the Atlantic to America. It followed them westward across this continent as the pioneers pushed their way to the Pacific.

In the same way it worked its eastward journey through Siberia, and China, and Japan — more slowly, perhaps, than under the influence of European and American hurry and enterprise, but just as constantly, and just as surely—till now, in friendly climates, it is a world-wide fruit.

*　*　*　*　*

Both of the pear trees described here, as in fact all of the pear trees which we know today, seem to have come from those common parents in eastern Europe or western Asia.

The one in Mr. Burbank's yard which bears the luscious fruit is the Bartlett pear—an excellent though common variety in the United States.

The other, with its bitter, indigestible fruit, is one which was imported from Japan.

*　*　*　*　*

The lesson which these two pear trees teach is that fruits, like flowers, in their rivalry to please us, adapt themselves to the tastes, desires, and ideals of the human neighbors among whom they grow.

[120]

A Chinese Lily

*The unusual shape of this flower, beautiful though it is,
shows how even flowers respond to the ideals of those whom
they grow to please. The very lines of this lily suggest dragons
and those other weird shapes which are pleasing to the eye
of the Oriental. This transformation in flowers was
worked in the same way that the transformation of
the pear, described here, was brought about.*

LUTHER BURBANK

Here, in America, we like fruits that are soft, large, sweet, luscious, juicy, aromatic, easy to digest when eaten raw. Our pears grow that way.

In Japan and China they like fruits which are hard, small, bitter, dry, acid—suitable only for pickling, preserving, or cooking. The Chinese and Japanese pear trees bear that kind of fruit.

Neither the Japanese pear, nor our American type, is like the original wild parent which was first discovered near the middle of Russia.

Each has changed — one toward one set of ideals—and the other toward another set.

* * * * *

If we could lay bare before us the whole history of the pear tree—if we could picture in our minds its stages of progress beginning back in the times, say, when instead of a fruit it bore only a seed pod like the geranium's—we should see a record of endless change, constant adaptation.

We should see that the soil, and the moisture, and the sunshine, and the air, throughout the ages, have played their parts in working the pear tree forward.

We should see that other plants, crowding it for room, or sapping the moisture from its feet, or adding richness to the soil by their decaying leaves and limbs, have done their share in hastening its improvement.

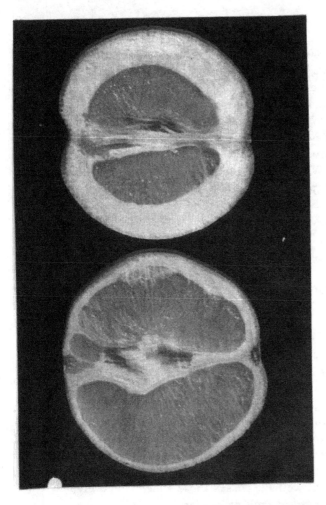

Less Rind, More Meat

*This color photograph print shows a good
comparison of the orange as it formerly grew and as
it grows today, since the orange has been transformed to meet our
ideals. Simply by selecting the kinds which have been
propagated this improvement has been worked.*

LUTHER BURBANK

We should see that the bees and butterflies and birds, with their help, and the caterpillars, locusts and deer in their efforts to destroy, have all served to aid the onward march.

We should see all the while a steady change for the better—sturdier pear trees, brighter blossoms, more seed, better fruit.

We should see that, with the aid of the elements, the pear tree adapted itself to exist, hardened itself to withstand many soils and many weathers.

We should see that, with the unintended aid of its plant and animal enemies, it gained strength through overcoming them.

We should see that, through the bees, it was helped into variation by mixing up heredities; and, by the birds, it was helped into still further variation by mixing up environments.

Then, overshadowing all of these influences, there came into its life new influences of man— man savage and civilized, Oriental and Occidental —man with a liking for pears.

Here in America, we who have grown pears have saved those which were the sweetest, the largest, the juiciest, the most luscious—because those were the ones we liked best.

When we have bought pear trees to plant in our yards, we have chosen those which would give us the kind of fruit we prefer.

ON ADAPTATION

The pear trees which have pleased us have received our care and cultivation—and we have multiplied them. The pear trees which have failed to produce fruit up to our ideals we have neglected and allowed to die—so that they have practically disappeared from our orchards.

The Orientals, their tastes and likes running in opposite directions from ours, have discouraged pear trees which bore the kind of fruit we prefer, and have selected, and saved, and fostered, and propagated those which gave them the hard, bitter fruit of their ideals.

And so the struggle for adaptation set in motion by the soil, the warmth, the cold, the moisture, and the winds, was supplemented by the bees, and then by the birds, until now we can read, in the result, our own influence and that of the Japanese.

* * * * *

There are differences between our dress and the dress of the Orientals; between our religions and the religions of the Orientals; between our ambitions and the Oriental ambitions; between our architecture and the architecture of the Orient —all reflecting the national or racial differences between the ideals of the two peoples.

And just as surely as the ideals of a people influence the architecture with which they surround themselves, just as surely as they change ambitions, mold religions, create dress styles, just so surely do they influence and change the characteristics of the plants in whose environment they live.

*　*　*　*　*

"When I say that man is the biggest element in the environment of plants," said Mr. Burbank, "I do not mean those few men who have devoted their lives to the improvement of plants. I do not mean the botanist, the horticulturist, the florist, the nurseryman, the agricultural experimentalist. I mean man in the mass—man busy with his dry goods store, or his steel company, occupied with his law, or his medicine, tired out from his daily blacksmithing, or his carpentering. I mean just man, the neighbor of plants, whether he be their friend or their enemy—whoever and whatever he is."

*　*　*　*　*

It was the savage Indian who gave us, here in America, the most important crop we have.

It was the Indian who found a wild grass covering the plains and developed it into corn.

Or, to turn it the other way around, it was the desire of the Indian for a food plant like this that led the teosinte grass, by gradual adaptation, to produce Indian corn or maize.

[126]

Our Corn and Its Tiny Parent

*In the direct color photograph print shown here a typical
ear of "dent" corn is placed for comparison beside the tiny teosinte
ear which the American Indians discovered and improved.*

LUTHER BURBANK

On Mr. Burbank's experiment farm there grows, today, this same teosinte grass which the Indians found.

It bears tiny ears with two rows of corn-like kernels, on a cob the thickness of a lead pencil, and two and a half to four inches long—slightly less in length and diameter than an average head of wheat.

From its earlier stage of pod corn, in which each kernel grew in a separate husk like wheat, teosinte represented, no doubt, a hard fought survival and adaptation like that of the flowering violet.

And when the Indians came into its environment it responded to their influence as the pansy responded to care and cultivation in its new dooryard home.

Where teosinte had formerly relied upon the frosts to loosen up the ground for its seed, it found in the Indians a friend who crudely but effectively scratched the soil and doubled the chance for its baby plant to grow.

Where it had been choked by plant enemies, and starved for air and sunlight by weeds, it found in the Indians a friend who cut down and kept off its competitors.

Where it had been often destroyed by the animals before its maturity, it found the selfish

Some Other Forms of Corn

*In the direct color photograph print shown here the
central ear and the ear at the right are "pod" corn, in which
each kernel is encased in a separate sheath. The ear at the left is
another form of teosinte with larger kernels than those in
the preceding print; from this latter the process by
which the kernels crowded each other until the cob
increased in size may be readily imagined.*

protection of the savages as grateful as though it had been inspired by altruism.

Planted in patches, instead of straggling here and there as best it could before, the teosinte grass found its reproduction problem made easier through the multitude of pollen grains now floating through the air.

And so, by slow degrees, it responded to its new environment by bearing more and bigger seed.

As the seed kernels increased in numbers and in size, the cob that bore them grew in length.

From two, the rows of kernels increased to four, to six, to eight, to fourteen.

Here again the selfish motives of the savages served to help the plant in its adaptation—for only the largest ears and those with the best kernels were saved for seed.

So, under cultivation, the wild grass almost disappeared, and in its place there came, through adaptation, the transformed Indian corn.

*   *   *   *   *

"There were two wealthy men in England," said Mr. Burbank, "who took up the daffodil and the narcissus, growing endless quantities of seedlings just for amusement.

"Both of these men, so it happened, were bankers. One was a rather large, coarse, strong, dominating type of man—not a repulsive man by any means, but lacking, a little, in refinement and the more delicate sensibilities.

"The other banker was a highly sensitive, nervous, shrinking man with a great eye for detail, a true appreciation of values, a man who looked beneath the surface of things and saw beauty in hidden truths, a man who thought much and said little.

"These men were great rivals in their daffodil- and narcissus-growing pastime, and each of them succeeded in producing some wonderful variations and adaptations in their plants.

"When these bankers died, their daffodil and narcissus bulbs were offered for sale and fell into the hands of a friend of mine, Peter Barr, a great bulb expert of England.

"Peter Barr told me that though the bulbs bought from those two estates were mixed and planted indiscriminately on his proving grounds, he could go through a field of those daffodils and narcissuses and, simply by the blossoms, tell which had come from one estate and which from the other.

"The flowers that came from the bulbs that represented the work of the first banker were large, coarse, brightly colored, virile, strong flowers—with a beauty that called to the passer-by as if out loud, and a self defiant attitude as if bespeaking an ample ability to take care of themselves.

"And the flowers which came from the bulbs produced by the other banker were charmingly delicate—not hardy, but rather shrinkingly artistic—not loud in their color schemes, but softly alluring with their subdued hues."

* * * * *

It costs money to ship oranges, so the more the meat and the less the rind, the less we waste in transportation charges.

A comparison of the wild orange with the cultivated fruit of our orange groves shows how this fruit has adapted itself to our ideas of economy.

* * * * *

Lettuce in the head makes a more appetizing salad than lettuce in large, sprawling leaves.

A comparison between wild lettuce and the head lettuce on our green grocer's stand shows plant adaptation to our salad demands.

* * * * *

And so with celery, and artichokes—and every plant that is grown for the market—wild, its adaptations are toward meeting wild environments; cultivated, its adaptations are toward fitting itself into our routine of life.

Wild Lettuce

A comparison between this and the large leaved, compact, salad plant of our gardens shows the wonders of adaptation which cultivation works. This wild lettuce is known in some places as the "compass plant" because of the fact that its leaves, instead of fanning out in all directions from the stalk, point always north and south—an adaptation, no doubt, to protect the plant from the heat of the mid-day sun.

Wild Celery

A comparison between this plant and the appetizing product which is found in our markets shows how we have taught the plant to give us straight, smooth, tender stalks, instead of the short, woody stalk, with long branches above it, shown here.

ON ADAPTATION

We have seen the price which variation costs; now we begin to see the value of it. Among those violets, environment—the environment of the present combining with heredity which is the recorded environment of all the past—contrived to see that there were no duplicates; that each violet, a little different from its mate, might, through its difference, be suited to a separate purpose, or fitted to carry a separate burden, or designed to fill a separate want.

If the violets had been as like as pins, they would have stayed as like as pins when planted in that friendly dooryard.

But because each had within it the power of transmitting variation, the power of responding, ever so little, to the trend of its surroundings, one violet became a pansy.

* * * * *

Among our human acquaintances we know those who are sturdy, and those who are weak; those who have well developed minds at the expense of their muscles, and those who have ell developed muscles at the expense of their minds, and those with a more evenly balanced development; we know some who are tall and some who are short; some with brown eyes and some with blue; some who lean toward commerce, and some who lean toward art; and on and on, throughout an infinite number of variations, an infinite combination of those variations, each variation representing the result of present environment reacting upon all of the environments of the ages, stored away.

As a people, we traveled by stage till the railroad came; and then in a single generation, because of the variation and the adaptability among us, we found surveyors to push their transits over the hills, and valleys, and streams; we found woodchoppers to make ties, we found steel makers who for the first time in their lives fashioned a rail, we found engineers, and firemen, and switchmen and superintendents, and railroad presidents, each to play his part in fulfilling the common desire for transportation, each able to adapt himself to new duties—and all because of this variation that is in us.

As a people, we submitted to a ruler across the seas till among our variant individuals there arose some who, different from the rest, adapted themselves to the formulation of a declaration of independence, the framing of a code of principles, the organization of a successful revolution.

As a people, threatened with the constant peril of cures which were worse than their diseases, there appeared out of the variable mass one who gave us antiseptic surgery.

ON ADAPTATION

Where are those who, a century ago, said that railroads could never be? Where are the Tories of revolutionary times? And where are those barbers of ancient days with their cupping glasses and their lancets and their leeches?

Ah, where are the pear trees of Eurasia that failed to fit into the scheme of adaptation—where are the geraniums that did not learn to advertise to the bee—and where are the desert cactus plants that could not protect themselves with thorns?

* * * * *

On and on we go, one step backward sometimes, then two steps forward—marking time awhile, then onward with a spurt—the pear tree, the geraniums, the cactus plants, and we—each individual among us a little different from the rest, each with a separate combination of old environment stored within us, finding always an infinity of new environment to bring it out; growing up together, the pear trees, the geraniums, the cactus plants and we, all of us depending on the others, and each of us playing his separate part in the forward march of adaptation.

On and on we go, because of Infinite Variation.

* * * * *

And so, from whatever viewpoint we approach the study of plants—whether with an eager eye to the future and the past, or whether with an

[137]

eye, opened only a slit, to see simply the things we can touch and feel, we find evidences of adaptation made possible through variation.

The violet, responding to kindness, became a pansy.

The pear, responding to racial tastes, adapted itself to the Orientals and to us.

Corn, responding to a need for food, produced forty times the kernels which it had produced before.

The orange, the lettuce, the celery, and every cultivated plant that grows, responding to our market demands, have transformed themselves to meet a readier sale.

And those daffodil and narcissus seedlings, how eloquently they tell of the adaptation of a plant to fit an individual ideal!

* * * * *

We studied electricity a long time without much apparent practical benefit. Then suddenly electric lights and trolley cars were everywhere.

We knew the principles of sound vibration for centuries before the telephone and the phonograph appeared, but it took less than a generation to make them universal.

We dreamed motor carriages three hundred years before we got one, and then, in a decade, we awoke to find our dream come true.

ON ADAPTATION

And almost from the beginning, man has studied the forces which go into the make-up of life without much encouragement, till now these ages of contemplation have begun to crystallize into thornless cacti, stoneless plums, fragrant calla lilies and a thousand other results as definite and as practical as the trolley or the telephone or the omnipresent touring car.

Who among us shall say what new plants even a decade, now, may bring forth?

—On and on we go; one step backward, sometimes; then two steps forward; marking time awhile; then onward with a spurt.

The African Orange Daisy

For the purpose of illustrating the practical methods of har-
nessing heredity, let us take the African Orange daisy and see if, from
the variations secured, we may not produce a new pink daisy.

Let Us Now Produce a New Pink Daisy

A Practical Lesson In Harnessing Heredity

AN architect, in selecting the materials for his structure, sends for limestone to Bedford, Indiana, or for marble to Carrara, Italy, or for bricks to Haverstraw, N. Y., or for redwood rustic to California.

In the process of turning his blue print into a building, he draws on the whole world—a little here and a little there—for his supplies.

So, too, in the production of a new plant on which we wish to try our architectural skill, we must first seek out the things with which to build.

Only our search will be not a search for substances, but a search for *stored up heredities*—not a search for bricks or stone or lumber, but a search for *living traits*.

* * * * *

The sturdy dandelions in our vacant lots, with their parachute-like seed balls, reveal a structural ingenuity and a fitness to survive which may have cost ten thousand generations of patient struggle.

The sweetness of our cherries, our grapes, our plums, has been developed only through ages and ages of response to environment, with some environments so oft repeated that they have hardened into heredity.

The flowers on our lawns may have acquired their colors in Germany, or in Ecuador, or in Siberia; our nuts reflect flavors picked up through a world-wide migration; and even our early vegetables show traits which hark back to times before animals and men came into their lives.

So, just as the earth has stored up limestone in Indiana, and marble in Italy, and brick-clay in New York, and ten-thousand-year-old redwoods in California, for the architect to draw upon, just so, in a world full of plants, representing an infinity of ancestry with its infinity of heredity, will we find an infinity of traits with which to build.

If we wish to change the color of a flower, or its scent, or its size, or its adaptability to climate— if we have it in mind to transform a tree or its fruit, or to give any plant a new trait or a new habit—the most practical way is to dig the quality we want out of the mass of heredity about us.

*   *   *   *   *

"I thought," says some one, "that plants could

[142]

be transformed merely by changing the environments in which they grow."

"So they can," replies Mr. Burbank, "if time is
no object. But the quick and economical way is
to take advantage of the combined environments
of the past which are at our instant disposal; to
short-cut to our result by using well established
traits and thoroughly formed habits, rather than
to spend the years or lifetimes which might be
necessary to produce new traits and new habits
from the beginning.

"It is better to seek out, first, what nature has
stored away for us, and then to use new environments to improve or intensify traits and habits
which already have the advantage of several
centuries of start.

"It is the same principle of economy which we
apply to everything we do.

"So long as there is plenty of coal within easy
reach it does not pay us to build machines to
utilize the energy of the sun's rays or of the ocean
tides. And, similarly, so long as there are untold
thousands of plants embodying, in some form,
almost every conceivable trait we might desire—
untold thousands of plants like the cactus waiting
only our attention to make them useful—we can
hardly afford to waste time in doing what nature
already, laboriously, has done."

LUTHER BURBANK

The hard part, always, is to make the start.

We who are late sleepers, for example, know the weeks of discouraging attempts it takes to fix the habit of arising at seven instead of eight, or at six instead of seven. Yet, once we have thoroughly accustomed ourselves to the new hour of awakening, it is just as difficult to get back to the old hour as it was to get away from it.

It is as if the tendencies within us, having accommodated themselves to each other and to our surroundings, cling together tenaciously to maintain the equilibrium between themselves; when we change our surroundings they adjust themselves to the change with difficulty; but once adjusted, hold together as firmly again as they held before.

So in plant life; when we transplant a flower or a tree, it shows signs, in accommodating itself to its new surroundings, of evident distress; it looks sickly, its leaves droop, it gives many outward proofs of the inward struggle which it is undergoing.

As soon, however, as its suddenly scattered tendencies have collected themselves, the plant begins an era of immediate improvement, and does as well or better than it did before transplanting—as well, in fact, as its new surroundings will permit.

ON HARNESSING HEREDITY

If new habits are hard to start, new traits are harder. It is hard to teach a plant to twine when it has never twined before, or to persuade it to be pink when it has always been yellow; just as it is hard to get a boy interested in the study of law when his likes, all his life, have been along the lines of engineering or mechanics.

In the establishment of a new trait, in fact, the whole motion of life must be interrupted, its momentum arrested, the resulting inertia overcome, and new momentum in a new direction gained.

But, if every difficulty has its recompense, we are well repaid for the labor of acquiring or instilling a new trait by the fact that, once acquired, it has a tendency of its own to increase and expand and grow.

The boy who finally gets interested in law, who gets past the point where it becomes an irksome drudgery, begins, at length, to develop a steadfast love for his work so that what was to him, once, a bug-bear at last becomes an absorbing ideal.

The cactus, for example, which produced its first spines with difficulty, now gets more and more spiny, although the need for spines has disappeared. Our flowers grow more beautiful, our fruits more luscious as their tendencies gain momentum.

We may take it as a rule, almost, that a habit, once fixed, hardens: that a trait, once established, grows stronger and stronger.

The easiest way, therefore, is to work *with* heredity, and not *against* it—to spend a month searching out a desirable trait or habit, rather than to spend a year or a decade trying to overcome an undesirable one.

* * * * *

And, now, to a practical experiment.

From almost any seed house we may procure the seeds of two African wild flowers. One is the African orange daisy, the other a white daisy of the same family.

The orange daisy is a sun-loving flower, as its beautiful, rich tint clearly testifies.

The white daisy, by its whiteness, shows equally unmistakable evidence of an ancestry which has preferred the shade.

"Bright colored flowers," said Mr. Burbank, "are almost invariably those which have grown in the sun. White flowers are either those which bloom at night, or which, if blooming in the day time, have stayed in the shade."

"Because the sun reacts with the soil to produce bright colors, while the shade does not?" was asked.

"No," replied Mr. Burbank. "I prefer to believe

that the bees make the colors. The flowers which grow in the bright light need their brilliance to attract the insects; flowers in the shade are more easily observed if they are light or white in color: it is all a matter of advertising contrast; and, throughout ages and ages, each particular flower has been striving to perfect a color contrast scheme of its own. It may be that the combination of sun and soil makes possible brighter colors than the combination of shade and soil; but wind-loving plants, like corn and trees, which grow in the sun, do not bedeck themselves in colors—only the flowers which find it necessary to attract the insects.

"In practice, at any rate, the color of a flower is one of the reliable guides in the study of its life-history."

Taking the orange daisy and its white cousin side by side, we see at once a family resemblance. The leaf formation, the root formation, the arrangement and the number of petals, the arrangement of stamens and pistils, bespeak the fact that here are two plants of a kind; one orange and one white; the white one taller a little, more graceful perhaps, and slightly less hardy; but cousins, beyond doubt, having within them many parallel strains of heredity.

Let us assume, then, that the orange of the

orange daisy is the heredity of ages of sunshine, and the white of the other daisy is the inheritance of ages of shade; that both started from the same point, and that one found itself growing in cleared fields, while around the other developed a forest of shade; so that, finally, as environment piled up on environment and accumulated into heredity, each flower became so firmly fixed in its own characteristics as to constitute a species, as man has chosen to call it, of its own.

If we take the seeds of the African orange daisy, and plant them in the shade, they will still produce orange flowers. That is stored up heredity. No doubt, if we continued, year after year, to replant them in the shade for a century or so, they would begin to transform themselves to white as the other daisy did.

If we plant the white African daisy in the sunshine, it will still give us flowers of white— the heredity of ages overbalancing the pull of immediate environment, and needing a long continued repetition of environment to balance and finally overcome it; but if we were to keep it in the sun throughout enough generations, it would, no doubt, bear us flowers of brilliant orange.

Here, then, is a single plant reflecting two divergent strains of heredity—one orange, one white — one sturdy, one weak — each strain so

We Find a White Cousin

Searching the African daisy family we perceive that one branch has been stranded from its kin and, finding itself in the shade, has become a white daisy. From the many similarities between the two flowers there can be no question that the white and the African orange daisy have a common ancestry—although some scientists classify them as different species, while some merely classify them as different varieties of the same species.

thoroughly fixed that in a lifetime it would be impossible, through pure environment, to over-throw it.

Let us next take a twenty-foot flower bed, say, divide it in the middle, plant one side solid with the orange daisies, and the other side solid with white daisies, and let the bees and the breezes mix those heredities up to produce for us the new pink daisy which we have planned to produce.

Up come the orange flowers, and up come the white. The breezes and the bees carry the pollen from flower to flower; the petals fall away, and disclose the pods of fertile seed in which, for the first time, these two strains of heredities are combined.

In the millions of seeds which we can beat out of these pods, there are some with the white tendencies stored away unaltered, some with the orange tendencies still predominant—some with white pulling evenly against orange to make a red, some with orange slightly stronger than white, and all of the infinity of variation in between.

We shall find in those seeds the mixed tendencies not only of the two species, but of all of the families of two species, and of the individuals of those families; mixed, upset, disturbed—so thoroughly that, not only will the life history of both parents be laid bare in the resulting plants,

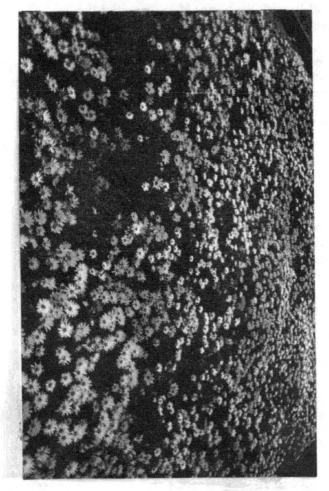

Having planted the seeds of the crosses between the two daisies we find a mass of flowers of various sizes and colors, with many surprising tendencies, from which to select. In this bed there are flowers which resemble each parent and which combine almost every blend of the parent characteristics, together with many characteristics which neither parent shows, but which take back to old heredity.

but through the blends, new characteristics, probably never seen before, will show themselves.

Here we have taken two plants which, since the beginning, have been storing up traits; each working out its own destiny; each separated from the other, perhaps by a mountain range or a lake, and thus never before brought to a place where those heredities could combine; then in a single season, through combination, we produce the seed for a new daisy reflecting every conceivable blend of those different heredities.

* * * * *

When we plant this seed the following spring, we shall have pure orange daisies and pure white daisies, pink ones, purple ones, yellow ones; daisies large and daisies small; daisies with big black centers, and daisies in which the centers are colored the same as the outside edges.

We shall find some a deeper orange than the orange daisy because the balance which has determined the established shade of orange has been upset.

We shall find purer whites than the white daisy ever knew—as a result of the upset.

We shall find daisies with petals whose color front and back is the same, and daisies with different colors inside and out.

We shall, in short, find all of the old inherit-

A Broadening of the Petals

*One of the first variations which we shall see in our bed
of crosses is the white daisy shown here in which the color of the
white parent is unchanged but which has broad petals
instead of the narrow ones of both parents.*

ances of the flower and of the combinations of them—all of the colors, scents if there be any, shapes, sizes, forms, elements of strength or weakness—uncovered before us.

And between the white and the orange we have but to select the particular pink flower of our fancy.

If the flower we select, perchance, showed some weakness, or if its tint were a little too light or too dark, or if for any other reason among this infinite color variation we did not find the exact result we sought, another season or another would surely bring it forth; for next year, instead of planting white and orange, we should plant a selection of our new daisies, and instead of getting a combination of two parentages, we should get a combination of combinations.

Then, having secured the color called for in our original mental blue print, we might find structural improvements to make in the flower— we might want to increase its height or to lengthen the daily period of its opening, or to rearrange its petals into a more chrysanthemum-like form, or to increase or decrease the size of its center — or to accomplish any one of a number of other ideals which we may have set up for our production.

So on we go, season after season, always

More Orange in the Center

*Selecting another white daisy from the patch we find the same broad
petals, but with a greater suggestion of orange in the center.*

selecting, getting one this year which bears a podful of seeds for next, with the bees and the winds anxious to carry on the work, narrowing our lines of heredity down and down and down, until finally some day—maybe fourteen months after the experiment began, or maybe fourteen years, we can say: "Here is a plant such as no man ever saw before—here is the exact plant which we have planned."

* * * * *

"But will the seed of this new pink daisy," some one asks, "produce more daisies of this same kind of pink?"

"Of all of the seeds of that daisy," says Mr. Burbank, "there might not be one which reproduced its parent pink. The seeds of that daisy sown together in a bed might easily show as great a variation as the seeds of the white and the orange showed when they were first planted after the bees and the winds had done their work.

"But that need be no discouragement. By dividing the roots of the daisy we can, in a single season, from a single plant, produce a whole bed of plants—each similar to the original plant because each, in fact, is a part of the original plant.

"We should, at the start, then, propagate our pink daisy by dividing the roots. We should

[156]

A Full Orange Center

*Looking still further into the white daisies
which we have produced we finally find one which has
a center of solid orange. If we were to take all of the
daisies from the patch we should find no two alike but an
almost infinite range of individual difference.*

find that for practical purposes it would thus be possible to produce all of the daisies we desired. We might never even care to make use of the seed. But if we did, by keeping our new pink daisies together year after year, in eight years, or perhaps ten or fourteen, pink being crossed with pink, and the upset equilibrium restored, we should find that we were getting seeds which came true, or nearly true, to type.

"You see, we upset heredity to produce variation; then we let it settle down to a balance to perpetuate the particular variation which we have chosen."

* * * * *

The architect can always build a second structure better than the first, and the plant improver, likewise, finds in each experiment a multitude of new suggestions for the production of still other changes or improvements.

In even the handful of daisy variations which can be reproduced here, there are to be seen countless new tendencies, any one of which might lead to the perfection of a wholly different, if not a better flower.

There are, of course, the variations in size— and those with the long petals show that with encouragement the flower, simply by quantity production and continued selection, might produce

More Evidence of Broad Petals

Taking up the orange and yellow daisies in the patch, we find the same tendency toward a broadening of the petal which, taking back to old ancestry, evidently, changes the appearance of the flower, as can be seen by comparing with the direct color photograph print on page 149.

an offspring with blossoms three inches or four or more in diameter.

There are, in the pictures shown here, some which indicate a tendency toward doubleness which gives rise to the thought that the new pink daisy, if desirable, might be entirely filled up with petals so that its center would not show at all, even as its very distant relative, the old maid's marigold, has been filled up—an interesting process which will be explained later.

Those daisies with the tendency toward darkened petals at the inner end might be cultivated and selected until finally they produced an offspring of a purplish black in the center with only a fringe of color, or, until the whole inside was solid black.

In other of the variations which are shown, it might be noted that some are pink, or yellow, or of colors in between, inside and out, while others show deep red or purple streaks on the backs of their petals. From these it might reasonably be expected to produce a daisy having one color within, and another color without.

From the bed of seedlings pictured, with no two daisies exactly alike, there might be prepared a list of a thousand different tendencies, each susceptible of cultivation, each the possible starting point of some new transformation.

A Better Orange Than Its Parent

*Looking further among the yellow flowers we find one
which has a more brilliant orange even than its parent. A
comparison between this plant and the one opposite page 158 will show
not only the difference in color, but the fact that this orange
daisy retains much of the gracefulness of its parent.*

LUTHER BURBANK

It is only when the life history of a plant, with all of its divergent tendencies, is uncovered in some such way as this, that the plant architect can see the full possibilities of further improvement.

* * * * *

The pink daisy which Mr. Burbank grew especially for the purpose of illustrating this chapter may, or may not, be a desirable production—it may or may not repay the thought and effort which it cost—but it shows the simplest method which the plant architect has within his reach—a method which, applied in the same way toward the accomplishment of a more utilitarian purpose, has meant and will, more and more, continue to mean, untold fortunes of added wealth to the world.

* * * * *

In order that the illustration may be complete, let us sketch some of the possibilities of employing this method.

Let us begin with some garden vegetable which for centuries has been picking up traits along the lines in which we have encouraged it—working away, always, from the wild, and toward the accomplishment of our ideals.

Let us say that we have been selecting it, unconsciously perhaps, for its tenderness, or sweetness, or early ripening, or productivity, or

Variation on the Outside

*In the same patch we find not only evidences
of heredity on the face of the flower, but on its back.
The bouquet pictured here shows, on the back of the petals, yellow
tendencies, greenish tendencies and even purple streaks
such as neither of the parents show.*

along any line which has made it more desirable or more marketable.

Its evolution, then, has been simply a slow response to a new environment which for the first time in its history included man.

Suppose, now, that we desire to work, in a single season or a dozen seasons, an improvement in this vegetable which will overshadow all of the improvement which countless generations of cultivation and unconscious selection have wrought.

Our first step is to secure its wild counterpart— inedible, maybe, sour, perhaps, tough, no doubt; wholly undesirable as compared with the plant which the seed bought at any grocery store will produce.

Nevertheless in the wild brother of our plant there is confined an infinity of old heredity just as an infinity of old heredity was confined in those two daisies; and the bees, and the winds, can bring forth variation between the tame and the wild, just as striking and just as widely divergent as the variations in the daisies.

Perhaps the first attempt to mix up the heredities of the tame and the wild might produce no improvement—only retrogression. But if we keep on mixing heredities and combining combinations of them, we shall soon see before us evidences of all of the tendencies of the plant—

We Could Make a Purple Daisy

*In our daisy patch we find one white daisy, unlike
the rest, with deep purple edges on the ends of its petals. If
we were in search of a purple daisy we might try the seed of
this, and from the variations resulting produce, at last, a
daisy which was all of the purple color shown here.*

tendencies which, though perhaps not desirable, point the way to an end worthy of accomplishment.

Then, instead of working with a single wild and a single cultivated plant, if we seek out a dozen wild plants or a hundred of them—some plants from mountain environments and some from swamps, some from rich woodland soil, and some from the desert, we shall get a still better idea of the possibilities stored within the plant—possibilities which need only combination and selection to bring forth a perfected product.

* * * * *

Or, suppose we have a tree which bears delicious fruit in small quantities.

Let us then find one with a tendency to overproduce, even though its fruit, in size, flavor and appearance, be inferior.

In some combination between the two, simply by following the leads which those combinations themselves will give, we shall in a few years, very likely, discover one variation which combines the productiveness of one strain of heredity with the deliciousness of another.

* * * * *

Or, perhaps, we have a plant which bears us berries of wonderful flavor, but too small to be marketable.

Let us find a plant with large, beautiful berries,

Our First Pink Daisy

Looking over the variations in our patch we discover one which has a dirty pinkish color. It is a step toward the end which we have started to achieve, yet is far from a satisfactory result. The petals are too broad and too stubby, and not evenly or gracefully arranged.

even though they be insipid, and see if, between the two, by matching heredities, there is not to be found some new berry which is luscious, large and beautiful.

* * * * *

Or, supposing that in our own particular soil there are varieties we should like to grow which fail to prosper, while other less desirable varieties do well.

Our problem then is but the combination of heredities to bring the desirability of one with the hardiness of another into a single new plant which, as it were, we make to order.

* * * * *

Or, if there is a variety which will not withstand the rigor of our winters, perhaps it can be combined with a poorer variety which has been educated to them.

Or, the other way around, if there is a plant which withers in the heat of our summers, perhaps some combination can be effected with an already existing brother or cousin, which, throughout the generations, has conquered the obstacle of heat.

* * * * *

And so on throughout the whole world-wide range of environment.

We shall find plants which have grown accustomed to the wet, and plants which are hardeι. .d

A Second Step in Selection

Looking further we find another pink daisy with longer petals, but too small a center, and still of a muddy color.

to the dry; plants which thrive in heat and plants which thrive in cold; plants which like sandy soil, and plants which can do well even in adobe clay; plants which have become used to the glare of the sun, and those which live retiring lives in the deepest recesses of the shade; plants which bear flowers large and small, early and late, of short seasons and of long, fragrant and unscented, simple and complex. We shall find fruit-flavors which are sour, sweet, acid, bitter; fruit skins which are smooth, fuzzy; fruits themselves that are large, small, even, irregular, coarse, delicate; we shall find those which will stand shipment across a continent and those which spoil almost as soon as they are picked.

We shall find a range of differences in wild plants, as great as the range of environments in which they have grown.

And we shall find a range of differences in cultivated plants as great as the range of differences in races and nations and individuals who have grown them.

* * * * *

"I saw an interesting illustration on the relation between heredity and environment at the circus one day," said Mr. Burbank.

"There, in a wire cage, was a tiny dog together with a lot of monkeys.

[170]

Try, Try Again

*With all of our pink daisies before us we find one,
now, with a center which is larger and more brilliant and
petals more nearly like those of the parent—slender
and graceful without seeming stubby.*

"While I was watching, a trainer appeared and snapped his whip.

"The monkeys quit their play with the dog, ran around in a circle, and climbed up the wire of the cage.

"The little dog followed them, but could not climb. He would start up and drop back, start up again and drop back again.

"Then he would look down at his feet, and if a dog ever showed surprise, that dog did. He seemed to be wondering why he could not climb as monkeys do.

"The environment was there, but the heredity was different.

"We see the same thing in plant life. The sweet peas with their tendrils and the nasturtiums with their leaves can climb like the monkeys, while other plants can not be forced to climb because there is no climbing heredity within them.

"You may try to make corn climb a hop pole, or to make hops grow straight in the air without a pole or string. But in a lifetime you can not succeed.

"It is heredity, heredity, heredity. Environment, unless oft-repeated, only serves to bring heredity out.

"The climbing monkeys and the disappointed dog show us an important truth in our work.

At Last the Pink Daisy

*From the pink variations which we have selected from our original
daisy patch, we finally, perhaps the first season, or perhaps the second,
secure a pink daisy of the same size, shape and gracefulness
as the orange daisy with which we started on page 140.*

"If we want to take advantage of a climbing tendency in a plant or an animal, let us by all means find a plant or an animal in whose heredity that climbing tendency is a part. Let us not try to teach monkeys to bark, or dogs to swing from the limbs of trees by their tails; let us not try to make corn climb the hop pole, or to transform hops into shade trees.

"Maybe these things could be done. In fact, with unlimited time, there is no question that they could be done. But with plenty of plants about us with ready-made heredities of which we can avail ourselves in a single season, it would be folly to try to accomplish the same result in a harder way, well knowing that only the twentieth or thirtieth generation ahead of us could see the results of our work.

"In our search for heredities we shall find many plants which are scarcely worth working with—plants whose environments have not led into heredities which are desirable for our ends.

"But at the same time we shall find scores and scores of plants in the least expected places—plants like the cactus, which, at first, seem impossible of use—which with a little encouragement yield us rare heredities for our work."

*　*　*　*　*

When the masons, and carpenters, and decorators have finished the architect's house, and the keys are turned over to the new owner—then, and from that moment, the structure begins to depreciate until it crumbles in decay. The furniture movers dent the stair rails, the children scratch the doors, dust begins to darken and destroy the lustre of polished surfaces; and the sun and night, and the frosts and the thaws, and the rain and the heat, slowly and irresistibly carry the structure on its downward grade.

But when the architect of plants has combined old traits into the production of his ideal, he has fashioned something which, if his work is well done, the suns, and the rains, and the frosts, and the winds will not depreciate; he has produced a living thing which, in spite of discouragements, and neglect, and abuse, will keep on, and on, and on—*improving as it goes.*

* * * * *

How few, indeed, are the materials which the architect of buildings has at his command, when compared with the range of living traits which the architect of plants may call into play!

—Our search, then, is a search for stored up heredities—a search for living traits.

Many Plants in Small Space

Visitors to Mr. Burbank's grounds often comment on the fact that in practically three acres most of his experimental work has been done; and with several thousand experiments continually under way, he has been asked why it is that the bees and birds, carrying the pollen here and there, do not disturb the crosses which he himself has made. The reason why this does not occur is explained in this chapter.

Short-cuts Into
the Centuries to Come

Better Plants Secured By
Hurrying Evolution

WITH the bees buzzing about in the thousands of blossoms on your experiment farm," said a visitor, "I should think that the plants would get all mixed up; I should think that the daisies would be crossed with carnations, and the carnations with balloon flowers, and the balloon flowers with poppies, and the poppies with cactus."

* * * * *

If we were to watch a bee at work, we should quickly discover one reason why this does not happen—one reason, at least, why the cherries, and the prunes, and the roses, and the geraniums have not long ago been reduced to a scrambled mess.

Our observation of the bee would show that, in going from flower to flower, it goes only to flowers *of a kind.*

[VOLUME I—CHAPTER VI]

We should see that, if it starts in the morning with clover, it visits no other blossom during the day but clover blossoms. Or if it begins on an orange tree, it passes the cherries, the peaches, the apples and anything else which may be in bloom, but will go miles to find orange trees; or if it starts on onions, then the geraniums and the carnations and the poppies have no attraction for it.

Which, by the way, is the reason that the bees produce, for themselves and for us, clover honey, and orange honey, and onion honey, each with a distinct flavor of its own.

But there are other reasons why the flowers do not get mixed up.

One is that while some flowers advertise to the bees, others advertise only to the humming birds —the bees can not get into the bird flowers and the birds can not get into the bee flowers; some flowers open in the early morning, and some toward noon; some bloom in April, and some in July.

The pollen granules of some flowers are so large that they can not push their tubes down into the egg nests of flowers with small pistils; there are structural differences between the various families of plants which seem to make cross pollenation almost impossible; and so on through a wide range of reasons why certain plants are

[178]

A Wide Range of Variation

This direct color photograph print shows a typical view on Mr. Burbank's experiment farm. The verbenas shown in this bed range from dark blue to light blue, from deep red to light pink, and represent a wide range of seedlings from which to select.

not readily mated with others—which will lead
us, in a later chapter, into the interesting study of
plant affinities.

* * * * *

The bees helped us to make a pink daisy
because, through heredity, the daisies of our first
planting gave daisy nectar, though their colors
were white and orange. And in seven out of any
ten experiments which we might try, we could
safely entrust the work of pollenation to the bees,
or birds, or other messengers with whom the
plants have built up partnerships.

But in those other three, the most important
of the ten, perhaps, we should find that the
pollenation would have to be done by hand.

If, for example, we desired to effect a combination between two flowers, one of which blooms in
the spring and the other in mid-summer, the
bees could be of no service. We should have to
take the pollen of the early blooming flower and
carefully save it until it could be applied to the
other.

If we desired to effect a combination between
a bird flower and a bee flower, even if in bloom
at the same time, we should find it necessary to
attend to the pollenation ourselves.

If we had it in mind to effect a cross between
a particularly large, insipid plum and a small,

highly flavored plum on another tree, or if we desired to effect a cross between any two *selected* parents, we should find it necessary to do our own work of pollenation.

*   *   *   *   *

It would seem that much of the ingenuity evident in nature is directed toward a two-fold end:

First, toward producing an endless combination of heredities in plants of the same kind—which, to give them a name, we may call crosses.

And second, to prevent the combination of things out of kind—which, to distinguish them from crosses, we may call hybrids.

The first aim ensures infinite variation—the mixing up of parallel strains of heredity in such a way that no two living things are exactly alike, and that, in each new balance of tendencies produced, there is the possibility of an improvement.

The second explains why, though all roses differ from each other, yet all are roses—why, though every living thing has its own individuality, its own personality, each bears the unmistakable characteristics of its kind.

*   *   *   *   *

"Here and there through nature, nevertheless, are hybrids. Are these accidents—the result of some carelessness, some lapse?"

[181]

LUTHER BURBANK

"In nature," said Mr. Burbank, "there are no accidents, no lapses. Everything that is, is a definite part of the Scheme of Things.

"We see crossing between kinds and realize its purpose, and see its value in the Scheme, because it is going on about us always, everywhere —because it is a quick-moving process which we can observe without doubt or difficulty.

"But when, on the other hand, we see the provisions in nature against crossing out of kind, those numberless ingenious devices designed to prevent the production of hybrids, we have no right to conclude that hybrids are not a part of the Scheme of Things.

"They are—else there would be no hybrids.

"Crossing between things of the same kind is a continuous, active process necessary to the production of better and better *individuals.*

"Crossing out of kind is a slower process which, I believe, has just as definite an end as crossing within kinds—excepting that its object, slowly and surely attained, is the production not of better individuals, but of better *kinds.*"

*   *   *   *   *

Let us go back to our African daisies.

If we read their history aright, there was, first, an orange flower which grew in the open veldt—a flower which accommodated itself to the

Another view on Mr. Burbank's experiment grounds showing a mass of Watsonias, thousands of them, set out and brought to bloom for the purpose of selecting possibly one or two.

peculiarities of the soil and the air in which it grew, and to its plant, insect, and animal neighbors —so that it became a thriving, successful race, each generation a little stronger—each year seeing it increase in numbers and spread in territory. In its spread, we may well imagine that the winds, or the animals, carried its seed over otherwise impassable barriers—just as human environment carries one son to New York to become a lawyer, another to Pittsburg to become a steel maker, and another to the gold fields of Nevada.

Thus reaching out, always into new environments, some branch of this daisy family found itself in the midst of a clump of trees—trees which multiplied and grew till they obscured the sun and left the tiny plants in the obscurity of dense shade.

As the trees grew (and just as slowly, quite likely), the daisies at their feet accommodated themselves to their new environment — they adapted themselves to the shade and moisture— they had less competition, perhaps, from other small plants and so became less sturdy—they changed their color to the one best suited to attract available messengers of reproduction.

At this point we interrupted the evolution of the African daisy by planting the white and the

[184]

orange together and securing, in the pink one, an immediate blend of their divergent heredities.

But it requires no stretch of the imagination to believe that, had we left them to their course, the same end would have been accomplished a century, or a thousand centuries, from now; that the same migratory tendency which took the white daisies into the woods would, in time, have brought them out of the woods and into the sunshine; or that the same tendency which got one division of the family into the woods would eventually have taken other divisions to the same woods; and that, sooner or later, there would have been white daisies growing alongside of orange daisies, so that, through the slow processes of nature, the same result which we produced by artificial means would have been achieved.

And so, in all of our experiments with plants, we shall find that we are not working *against* evolution, but *with* it; that we are merely providing it with short-cuts into the centuries to come—short-cuts which do not change the final result, but only hasten its accomplishment.

And who shall say that we, helping our plants to do in 1913 what without our help they might not be able to do before 3913—who shall say that we are not elements in evolution just as the bees, and the birds, and the butterflies, and the winds, and

[185]

Seedlings—I

From this print it will be seen that Mr. Burbank first plants his seedlings closely in a shallow box. These boxes or "flats" are about eighteen inches square and two or three inches in height. No two of the seedlings, of coarse, are exactly alike, and from these Mr. Burbank makes his first selection. The box or "flat" at the right contains one hundred cactus seedlings; the "flat" at the left contains four hundred.

the rains, and the frosts—who shall say that
our influence, inestimably greater than any other
influence in the life of a plant—is not an intended
part of progress in the Scheme of Things?

    *   *   *   *   *

In hurrying evolution, we can, and do, play a
more important part, even, than that of bringing
about crosses, or hybrids, which the bees or the
birds would never make.

The greatest service which we render toward
the advancement of plant life is that of selection,
endless, skillful selection.

The pink daisy was really, after all, the result,
principally, of selection. The important thing we
did was not to bring a mass of daisies together
for the bees to work on; the important thing was
to select orange daisies, and white daisies, with
the *purpose* of producing a pink one. Then, with
a bedful of variations, we selected again—selected,
this time, for the shade we wanted, and destroyed
the rest.

Afterward, with that pink daisy, we began
a still further course of selection, selecting the
largest, the hardiest, the tallest; and no matter
how long we might continue to grow pink daisies,
we should keep on selecting, selecting, selecting—
each step in our selection, because it has the
human mind behind it—because it is actuated by

Some Cactus Seedlings—II

*After making his first selection from the "flats," Mr. Burbank
transplants his seedlings in the ground, as shown. From the
time the seedling first shows its head until the final object is
achieved, there is selection, selection, constant selection. The
points for which he watches in his process of selection are
clearly explained in the treatment of each specific subject.*

purpose an͜ ͜esire—each step in this selection
representing ͜ ͜. advance, which, without our help,
might take a hundred or a thousand years to
bring about.

So, in working out any ideal in plant improvement, the first factor and the last one is selection.
Selection enters into the ideal itself, it enters into
every step of its accomplishment, and it enters
into the production of every succeeding plant
which represents that accomplishment.

*   *   *   *   *

"If you believe that nature makes no mistakes,
and has no lapses, how can you account for the
evident unfitness of so many individual plants
to survive — how can you account for the
wastefulness and extravagance which is apparent
throughout all forms of plant life?"

"Leaving nature out of it for the moment,"
replied Mr. Burbank, "let us look at the work
which I have been doing here for forty years.
There has hardly been a time during this period
when I have had less than twenty-five hundred
experiments under way, and there have been
seasons when from three to five thousand were in
process. I estimate that, right on this three
acre tract, considerably more than one hundred
thousand definite, separate experiments in plant
life have been conducted, in all.

LUTHER BURBANK

"Some of the experiments which have taken the most time and cost the most money have produced no apparent result; and some of the results which seem most important have been achieved in the simplest way, with the least expenditure of effort.

"Out of the entire total of experiments tried, there have been not more than two or three thousand which, so far, have resulted in a better fruit, or a better flower, or a more marketable nut, or a more useful plant.

"On the other hand, I should feel repaid for all the work I have done if only a dozen of my experiments had turned out to be successes. It is the nature of experimentation—we must try many things in order to accomplish a few.

"And this is just exactly what is going on in nature all the time—excepting that where we might get one success out of forty failures, there might be but one out of a thousand or a million if the plants were left to work out their own improvement, unaided.

"Then, after all, the unsuccessful experiments are failures only in a comparative sense.

"If you have ever watched the bridge builders constructing a concrete causeway, you must have seen the false construction which was necessary— the stout wooden structure into which the plastic

Mr. Burbank at Work

In the foreground of this print it will be seen that three of the flowers are separated from the rest by being tied with white string. As he goes about his gardens, Mr. Burbank picks out those flowers which come nearest his ideals and marks them thus that their seed may be saved. The entire process of marking and recording not only flowers but all other plants will be explained in the proper place.

material was poured—a costly structure in itself
which was put up only to be torn down.

"We can not call this wooden structure extravagance or waste, because it was a necessary step
in the completion of the work. And so, while,
in nature, we find many individuals which are
weak—many steps which look like backward
steps instead of forward ones—many apparent
oversights, yet I prefer to believe, and my own
work has shown me that this is true, that these
are simply elements in a necessary scheme of
false construction, without which the final object
could not be achieved.

"The price of all progress is experiment; successful experiment is brought about, always, at
a terrific expense of individual failures.

"But who shall say that progress, any progress,
is not worth all it costs?"

* * * * *

Nature gets one success out of a million tries;
Mr. Burbank has gotten one out of forty. The
figures may not be exact, but the basic fact
underlying them is none the less important.

It was simply by eliminating steps and providing short-cuts, and bringing the human mind
with its ideals, will, judgment and persistence into
the environment of the African daisy that we were
able to produce a pink one in a few months when,

without our influence, nature might easily have taken till 3913.

* * * * *

The real work before us, then, is to study nature's processes—to learn to read the history of plants, to uncover tendencies and understand their trends—and then to provide short-cuts so that the far distant improvement may be made a matter of months, instead of centuries.

These short-cuts, and their application, from this point on, will be our principal study; perhaps a single illustration here, more comprehensive than that of the daisy, will serve to give a clearer idea of their kind:

Let us take, then, as a specimen, Mr. Burbank's methods in the production of a new cherry.

First, as with the daisy, there must be an ideal —some particular kind of cherry of which we have made a mental blue print. Let us say that our blue print calls for a large, sweet cherry, which will ripen early and bear long—an eating cherry rather than a canning cherry, so that appearance is a great factor.

The first step would be to gather in our elements; to pick out a large, beautiful cherry which, after the manner of many large, beautiful fruits, may be more or less insipid in taste; then to select another cherry, size and appearance inconsequential, which has the delightful flavor our plans and specifications call for.

Let us take not one of each of these types, but a number of them, and then when they have bloomed, let us, by hand, cross them back and forth, making in all, we will say, five hundred crosses; each tied with a certain color of string for the purpose of later identification.

The petals of the blossoms which we have crossed will fall away; long stems bearing green cherries will begin to take their place; and finally, the twigs which we have marked with strings will tempt us with their ripened fruit.

* * * * *

There is an interesting legend of the French girls who used to take apple boughs in blossom and shake the pollen over the apple flowers of another tree, a legend of the wonderful variation in the apples which they secured.

And here and there in our work we shall see exceptions to the general rule, which seem to prove that the French legend perhaps was founded on fact.

These exceptions, which will form the basis of an interesting series of experiments for us later, need have no bearing on our present cherry work.

For, as a matter of practical fact, we shall find no outward evidence of our work. The meat of the five hundred cherries which we have crossed, we can safely assume, will taste the same, and be the same, as though we had let the bees attend to pollenation; the cherries that result will be no different in flavor or appearance than the other cherries on the tree.

But inside the stony seed of each of those cherries we shall find an indelible living record of what we have done.

So, disregarding the fruit, we save our five hundred cherry seeds and plant them in a shallow box until they have sprouted and then transplant them till they attain a six or eight inch growth.

*   *   *   *   *

So far, let us see how we have shortened nature's processes.

In the first place, we have brought together a large, insipid cherry and a homely, small, sweet one, brought them from points, perhaps, two thousand miles apart.

In the natural course, those two cherries would have spread; they would, eventually, have come together, no doubt; but we have brought them together without delay. Perhaps, in this, we have saved a thousand years.

In bringing our two kinds of cherries together we have brought not only one of each type, but dozens, or hundreds, each selected for its size,

In all of his experiments, Mr. Burbank tries to crowd his variations close together so that comparisons may be more easily made and the process of selection thus facilitated. This tulip bed illustrates the idea.

or appearance, or some probable quality which it contains within. In this simple selection of individuals we may have saved other thousands of years.

With unerring accuracy we have seen that the pollen of the two kinds has been interchanged, so that the five hundred or so resulting seeds will represent the two heredities we wish to mix—and only these.

Who can estimate how long it might have taken the bees and the winds, working even in neighboring trees, to effect specific crosses with the certainty which we have assured?

Now, with new heredities bundled up in our five hundred cherry stones, we plant them under every favoring condition in our shallow box, and unless mishap or accident intervenes, we get new cherry trees from all, or, at worst, lose but a few.

From five hundred other cherries on a tree, leaving the birds to distribute the seed, how many seedlings will there sprout?

* * * * *

And now, with our sprouted cherry seedlings six inches or eight in height, with no man knows how many thousand years of nature's processes cut out, we come to the most important short-cut of all—quick fruiting, so that there may be quick selection.

LUTHER BURBANK

Grafting is no new practice.

Virgil wrote verses about it:

But thou shalt lend
Grafts of rude arbute unto the walnut tree,
Shalt bid the unfruitful plane sound apples bear,
Chestnuts the beech, the ash blow white with the
pear,
And, under the elm, the sow on acorns fare.

Pliny, within the same century, describes a cleft graft and bespeaks the following precautions: that the stock must be that of a tree suitable for the purpose; that the cleft must be taken from one that is proper for grafting; that the incision must not be made in a knot; that the graft must be from a tree which is a good bearer, and from a young shoot; that the graft must not be sharpened or pointed while the wind is blowing; that the graft should be inserted during the moon's increase; with the final warning, "A graft should not be used that is too full of sap, no, by Hercules! no more than one that is dry and parched."

*   *   *   *   *

"Graft close down to the trunk," the later theory of grafting has been, "there the sap pressure is highest and the grafted cion has the best opportunity to live.

"Graft away out at the tip ends of the tree," thought Luther Burbank, "and you will save from two to seven years of time."

[198]

ON HURRYING EVOLUTION

It was the same kind of observation as that which led to the production of a spineless cactus; the same keen eye for cause and effect which showed Luther Burbank a new theory of grafting —which opened the way to a practice which makes possible, comparatively, immediate results.

＊　＊　＊　＊　＊

Grafting close to the trunk gives the cion a better chance.

"Give anything a good chance," thought Mr. Burbank, "and it takes its own time to mature.

"Take away that chance, and responding to the inborn tendency of every living thing to reproduce itself, it will hasten the process without waiting to accumulate strength. Therefore, if we graft away out at the tip ends of the tree, while we make it harder for the cions to exist, yet, in consequence, they will bear us quicker fruit.

"Furthermore, if we graft close to the trunk we can, at best, attach but six, or eight, or a dozen cions.

"But if we graft out at the tip ends, we can put five hundred cions on a single tree."

＊　＊　＊　＊　＊

Grafting was nothing new; but it remained for Luther Burbank to learn the secret of producing, by means of it, five hundred different kinds of fruit on a single tree at the same time, so that a comparative test might be made. It remained for Luther Burbank, with his theory of starving a living thing to make it hasten its reproduction, to cut from two to seven years out of the long wait for the fruit which is to tell the story of the heredities which were confined within the seed.

It is possible, at this point, to give but the barest glimpse of the results which Mr. Burbank's improvements in grafting have made possible. Under the proper heading the details of method will be fully explained, together with a summary of the results of hundreds of thousands of grafts, showing that, while the average time of fruiting has been brought down to less than two seasons, in some exceptional cases Mr. Burbank has secured fruit for testing the *same season that the graft was made.*

Here, too, it is not possible to convey more than a general idea of his plans which, in every operation, are aimed toward the end of producing the quickest possible test. Whether it be the quince seedlings bearing fruit in six months; or three-foot chestnut trees loaded down with nuts; or twelve year old walnut trees, the size of their seventy year old cousins—all through this work the plan and the method is to save time for the *individual plant* as well as to provide short-cuts for the process of evolution.

An Apple Graft One Year Old

As evidence of the success of Mr. Burbank's methods of producing quick results, the apple graft, in full bearing, after only one year's growth, speaks eloquently.

LUTHER BURBANK

To go back to our cherry seedling, now six inches above the ground, if we were to depend on nature's processes, by careful planting and cultivation we might produce cherries in seven years; but by short-cutting through grafting, and short-cutting grafting itself through Mr. Burbank's plan, we shall have our cherry crosses in 1914 instead of in 1920—five hundred of them all on a single tree, so that they can be plucked and laid out, first, for a visual selection, to pick out the ones which conform to our ideas of color, and size, and beauty; and, second, for selection through taste—to find the one, or the two, or the dozen among them which come nearest the ideal of our original mental blue print.

Perhaps of the five hundred cherries spread before us, none may fit the blue print; or perhaps one or two, approximating it, may show signs of further improvements which ought to be made.

Eliminate the rest, and start afresh with those two—begin at the very beginning with them again—mix up their heredities with other desirable heredities from near or far, grow seedlings, produce quick fruit through grafting, and select again.

* * * * *

Every little bit Mr. Burbank has, as the neighbors choose to call it, a $10,000 bonfire.

A Chestnut Graft One Year Old

*One year before this picture was taken the heavily laden
branch of chestnuts seen above was a seedling with its possibilities
unknown. In the brief span of twelve months Mr. Burbank
has now before him the chestnuts which are to
be the proof of the success or failure
of his experiment.*

A Burbank Bonfire

The photograph print here is remarkable in that it is made from a color photograph taken at night of one of Mr. Burbank's so-called $10,000 bonfires. Such a photograph in even black and white would be extremely difficult of accomplishment.

ON HURRYING EVOLUTION

In such a bonfire there would be 499 cherry grafts out of the five hundred which we have just made; there would be 19,999 rose bushes which had been brought to bearing in order to find the twenty thousandth which was not burned—or perhaps twenty thousand rose bushes, the one sought for not having been worth the saving; there would be 1,500 gladiolus bulbs with an easy market value of a dollar a piece, put in the fire after the one, or the two, or the dozen best among them had been selected; there would be a thousand cactus seedlings, representing three years of care and watchfulness, but useless now, their duty done. A ten thousand dollar bonfire, indeed, without exaggeration.

The builder of bridges can sell the lumber used in his false construction for seconds; and so, too, could Mr. Burbank profitably dispose of the elements of false construction in his work—those millions of seeds and bulbs and cuttings which represent second bests or poorer; but he does not; every step in the process excepting those concerning the final result is obliterated with a ruthless hand.

"It is better," says Mr. Burbank, "to run the risk of losing a perfected product, through the destruction of the elements which went into it, than to issue forth to the world a lot of second

bests which have within them the power of self
perpetuation and multiplication, and which, if we
do not destroy them now, will clutter the earth
with inferiority or with mediocrity."

So, we see that, while nature eventually would
produce the things which we hurry her to produce,
yet the improvements would find themselves in
competition with the failures which they cost, the
failures outnumbering the improvements, perhaps,
a million to one. We see that we not only shorten
the process, not only achieve a result out of every
forty failures instead of every million, but we give
our product the advantage of a better chance to
live—we remove from it the necessity of fighting
its inferiors for the food, and air, and sunlight
which give it life.

* * * * *

This, then, is the story of the making of a new
cherry to fit an ideal:

First, selection of the elements; second, combining these elements; third, bringing these combinations to quick bearing; fourth, selecting one
out of the five hundred; and then, selection, on
and on.

Interesting and wonderful as the process of
pollenation is, ingenious and successful as Mr.
Burbank's method of grafting is, important and
highly perfected as his methods of growing and

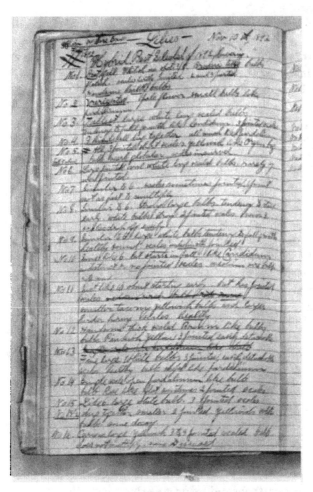

One of Mr. Burbank's Records

*This page from one of Mr. Burbank's record books gives
an indication of the careful, painstaking manner in which he
has recorded all of his experiments. With seeds, bulbs and slips
coming to him continually from all over the world; and with
more than forty years of work recorded, these books
form now a large and interesting library.*

caring for seedlings are—these, after all, are but details in the process—minor details, in fact.

The big element, over-towering them in importance, is selection.

First, the selection of an ideal, then the selection of the elements which are to be blended to achieve it, then the selection of the resultant plant, and after that the selection of better and better individual plants to bear the fruit which reproduces the original selected ideal.

* * * * *

Everything we do, then, is simply done to facilitate selection.

We produce new plants in enormous quantities, in order that there may be many from which to select; and having selected, we destroy nine hundred and ninety-nine one thousandths of our work.

We strive all the while to produce quick results—to eliminate the long waits and to shorten those that we can not wholly eliminate—simply so that our selection may be truly comparative—as that of five hundred fruits tasted in a single afternoon, and so that lingering expectancy may not prejudice our judgment, or the result.

* * * * *

It took two thousand years to bring about the juicy American pear by unconscious selection—

Five Hundred
Kinds on One Tree

This direct color photograph print shows Mr. Burbank's famous cherry tree on which he has produced as high as five hundred kinds of cherries at the same time—this for the purpose of easy comparison and intelligent selection.

and two thousand years for the Orientals to produce the pear they liked.

Yet, as plant improvement goes, the pear was quick to respond to its environment; other fruit improvements wrought through unconscious selection have taken ten times as long.

On the other hand we see Luther Burbank's cherry tree, bearing more than five hundred different kinds of cherries at the same time, cherries produced to compare with a mental blue print less than three years old—cherries, from among which, one, at least, will be found, which will lead the way to the achievement of the ideal.

And, similarly, in every department of plant life, whether it be in farm plants, or garden plants, or forest plants, or lawn plants, or orchard plants, or whether it be in plants which we grow for their chemical content, or for their fibers, or what—we shall find that it is possible to devise short-cuts into the centuries to come, and through combining stored up heredity with new environment, to hurry evolution to produce for us entirely new plants to meet our specific desires.

—Who shall say that progress, any progress, is not worth all it costs?

How Far Can Plant Improvement Go?

The Crossroads—Where Fact and Theory Seem to Part

W HEN I first began this work," said Mr. Burbank, "I was taught that a combination between two varieties of the same species was possible—that I might cross one plum with another plum, for example, to get a new variety—but that the species marked the definite boundary within which I might work. The science of that day was firm in its belief that a seed-bearing, self-reproductive cross between plants of different species was beyond the pale of possibility.

"A little later on, when I succeeded in combining the plum with the apricot, and produced, thereby, a new fruit whose parents were of undeniably different species, the law, or rule, was moved up a peg; and I was told that while it might be possible to effect combinations between different species, yet that must be the limit of

This direct color photograph print shows Mr. Burbank's plumcot, which, aside from the fact that it is one of the most luscious of fruits, entirely new and different in appearance and flavor, is of great interest because it represents a combination between two species—the plum and the apricot—which up to the time of the production, scientists had believed could never be made.

accomplishment; that combinations between the next higher divisions, genera, were beyond the power of man to effect.

"Then, when I was able, after a time, to take parents of two different genera, like the crinum and the amaryllis, or the peach and the almond, or a score of others which might be mentioned, and to effect successful seed-producing combinations between them, I began to hear less and less about laws and rules.

"The fact is that the laws and the rules are all man-made.

"Nature, herself, has no hard and fast mode of procedure. She limits herself to no grooves. She travels to no set schedule.

She proceeds an inch at a time—or a league—moving forward, always, but into an unmapped, uncharted, trackless future.

"I like to think of Nature's processes as endlessly flowing streams; streams in which varied strains of heredity are ever pouring down through river beds of environment; streams which, for ages, may keep to their channels, but each of which is apt, at any time, to jump its banks and find a different outlet.

"Just about the time we decide that one of these streams is fixed and permanent, there is likely to come along a freshet of old heredity, or

The Amaryllis and Its Parents

*Having effected a combination between species, Mr. Burbank,
in the amaryllis, made a combination between genera. In this
direct color photograph print the improved amaryllis and
its tiny parents are shown in truthful proportion.*

between genera Mr.
B u r b a n k continued his
work with the amaryllis
until he finally produced
flowers like those shown
h e r e, almost a foot in
width. The color range is
remarkable, extending from
pure white to deep red
with countless won-
derful variations
in between.

Still Another Amaryllis

This direct color photograph print shows an entirely different form of amaryllis which Mr. Burbank improved by crossing out of kind. This flower often reaches a diameter of eight inches and with its long, richly colored, drooping petals, it is one of the most admired of his flower productions.

a shift in new environment; after which we must rebuild our bridges and revise all our maps."

* * * * *

Since the subject of classification is an important one; and since Mr. Burbank upsets some man-made law or theory on an average of about once in every sixty days, it may be well, at this point, to take a bird's-eye glimpse over the maps and charts which have been worked out.

With a subject in which the bulk of truth is masked in the obscurity of past ages, and with many men of many minds attacking it from many viewpoints, it is only to be expected that there should be differences of opinion.

But, for the sake of making the explanation clear, we may, for the moment, overlook minor divergences and view, only, the main backbone plan which meets with the broadest acceptance.

To begin at the beginning, we see, first, spread before us, three kingdoms, whose boundary lines are well surveyed, and whose extent is all-inclusive. These, as our Duffy's second reader told us, are the mineral, the animal, and the vegetable kingdoms.

Our interest lies now in the vegetable kingdom, which divides itself into six (perhaps seven) branches, or subkingdoms, called phyla.

The lowest of these subkingdoms includes

[217]

only those vegetables of the simplest type which reproduce by splitting themselves in two. In this subkingdom live the death-dealing bacteria, which bring about such human diseases as tuberculosis and malaria, or such plant diseases as black rot; and the good bacteria, too, which are everywhere, helping us to digest our food, and without whose help the higher subkingdoms of plant life could not exist; and other plants of the same grade.

The next subkingdom, higher by a step, includes the yeast which we use to raise our bread, or those microscopic vegetables which turn hop juice into beer, apple juice into cider and rye juice into whisky; and others. Those who prefer to chart seven subkingdoms instead of six, divide this branch into two, making the slime-molds a separate phylum.

The next subkingdom, ascending the scale, includes, among others, the mosses and liverworts.

From these it is but a step to the next subkingdom, which includes the ferns—the highest type of flowerless plants, and the first, in the ascending scale, to exhibit a complete development of root, stem and leaf.

The final subkingdom, and the one into which our work principally takes us, embraces those plants which produce seeds.

ON FACT VS. THEORY

Taking, then, this latter, the highest sub-kingdom, we find that it separates into two broad divisions, called classes, one of which is distinguished by bearing its seeds in enclosed packages called ovaries; the other bearing seeds which are exposed, or naked. The first of these classes includes the vast majority of seed-bearing plants; the other including principally those trees, like the pine and the cypress, which bear their seeds in open cones.

Next, on our chart, we shall find that the class is subdivided into orders. The order represents a collection of related families. As an example, the order *Rosales* is made up of the rose family, the bean family, the cassia family, the mimosa family and twelve other families closely allied.

Below the order comes the family—a division which is still broadly inclusive; the rose family for example taking in not only the rose, itself, but the apple, the blackberry and sixty-two other plants whose close relationship might not at first be evident.

From the family we next narrow down to the genus—which separates the rose from the apple and the blackberry and gives each its own classification.

Beneath the genus there comes the species.

And beneath the species the variety.

We may take it as a safe observation that the simpler the form of life, the less the tendency toward variation; the more complex, the greater the opportunity for individual differences.

So, in the simpler subkingdoms, and in the more general divisions down to and including the order, the lines of division are more readily differentiated, and the work of classification has been fairly free from quarrels.

But as the order breaks up into families, and the family breaks up into genera, and the genus breaks up into species, and the species breaks up into varieties, and variations tend more and more to carry the individual away from its kind, there are to be found dissentions and differences of opinion which could hardly be chronicled in twelve full volumes of this size.

*   *   *   *   *

Nor is this divergent opinion surprising.

It is said that, of an iceberg floating in the sea, but one-eighth is visible to the surface observer, while seven-eighths of the mass are submerged beneath the water line.

Who, from looking at the one-eighth in view, could be expected to draw an accurate detail picture of the iceberg as a whole?

The vegetable kingdom which presents itself to our vision today has been under observation, at most, but a few hundred years. It has behind it, who shall say, how many tens of thousands of generations of ancestry which, coming before man, went by unobserved—yet which, under new environment, are continually bursting forth to confuse us.

How can man, with only one ten-thousandth of his subject revealed to him, be expected to make charts or maps which shall withstand onslaught, or be superior to criticism?

*   *   *   *   *

For the sake of ready understanding, we may, however, summarize plant life into the broad classifications outlined above.

First, the vegetable kingdom, which includes all plants.

Second, the subkingdom or phyla, six or seven in number.

Third, the class, which ranks above an order and below a phylum.

Fourth, the order, which ranks between the class and the family.

Fifth, the family, which ranks below an order but above the genus.

Sixth, the genus, which ranks below a family but above the species.

Seventh, the species, which ranks below a genus and above the variety.

Eighth, the variety, which ranks below a species and above the individual.

Yet with but *one certainty* in the entire scheme of classification—that certainty being the individual, itself.

Men may tell us that a plant belongs to one genus or to another, that it is of this species, or of that—or that it is even of a different family than at first we thought—but these, after all, are but theories, built up about the plant by man—theories which serve merely as guide posts in our work.

The plant itself, the *individual plant,* if we but watch it and give it an opportunity to show, will tell us for itself, beyond dispute or denial, just what manner of plant it is—just what we may hope for it to do.

*   *   *   *   *

Next in importance to classifying plants, from a superficial standpoint, is a method of naming them.

When we go to the florist's we ask for roses, or marigolds; when we go to the fruiterer's we talk to him of oranges, and plums, and cherries; when we go to the green grocer we ask for lettuce, or cabbage, or peas; when we select furniture we talk of it as being made of mahogany, or oak, or walnut.

ON FACT VS. THEORY

Thus, commonly, we call all forms of plant life by their nicknames—and by their nicknames only do most of us know them.

One reason, likely enough, is that the scientific names of plants are in Latin—for the good reason that the Russian, or Swedish, or Spanish, or American scientist is able to describe his work, thus, in a common language.

In giving a plant its Latin name, no attention is paid to its class, order or family.

The name of the genus becomes its first name.

The name of the species follows.

And the name of the variety, when given, comes last.

Thus, in writing the scientific name for an apricot, or a plum, or a cherry, we should give first the name of the genus, which, for all of these, is *Prunus.*

If we are to describe, for instance, a cherry of the species *Avium*, we should write, following the name of the genus, the name of the species, as *Prunus Avium.*

And then, if we were to write the name of some particular improvement in that species of cherry which Mr. Burbank had wrought, say the famous Burbank cherry, we should follow the names of the genus and the species with the name of that variety, as *Prunus Avium Burbank.*

[223]

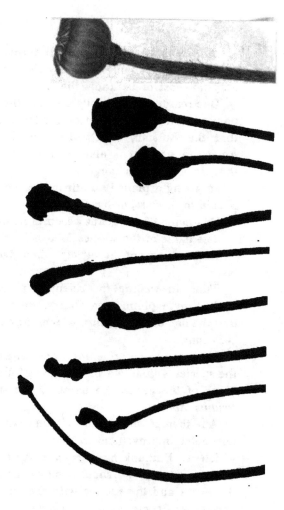

The capsules of second generation hybrid poppies shown here illustrate a wide range of variations from complete absence of capsules to capsules of unusual size. These were selected at random from about two thousand plants.

ON FACT VS. THEORY

Or, if we were to prepare a technical article, about this species, we should write *Prunus Avium* at the first mention of it, and contract it to *P. Avium* when mentioning it thereafter.

In this work, in order to gain clearness with the least effort, and to avoid confusion through the use of disputed terms, it has been decided, so far as possible, to call plants by their commonest names; going, wherever necessary, into a brief explanation in order to identify the plant clearly in the mind of the reader.

Our work is to be a practical work, and the effort which it would cost to master thousands of Latin names might, it is believed, be better expended in a study of the principles and the practice.

There arises, unfortunately, a confusion through use of common names. The California poppy, for example, is not a poppy at all; but for the purposes of this work it has been deemed best to call it the California poppy, by which name it is generally known, rather than to refer to it as *Eschscholtzia;* and so on throughout the list of other plants.

No common name is used, however, which is not to be found in the dictionary; so that those whose scientific interest is uppermost have but to refer to their Webster, which gives a greater wealth of detail than could be hoped for in a glossary or an appendix to these volumes.

* * * * *

"A few years after I came to Santa Rosa," said Mr. Burbank as he was sitting on his porch one evening, "I was invited to hear a new minister preach on a subject which, I was assured, would be of interest to me.

"It was not my own church, so I tried to find my way to an unobtrusive seat in the rear, where I should disturb no one. But, as if by prearrangement, the usher would not have it that way—I was led to the front center, where I was given a pew to myself.

"As soon as the sermon began, I saw the reason for it all. That preacher, with a zeal in his heart worthy of a better cause, had evidently planned a sermon for my own particular benefit. He was determined to show me the error of my ways.

"He began by describing 'God's complete arrangements' as evidenced in the plants about us, and rebuked me openly for trying to improve on the creations of Omnipotence. He held me to ridicule as one who believed he could improve perfection; he predicted dire punishment for attempting to thwart Nature and tried to persuade me, before that audience, to leave God's plants alone.

[226]

The Primus Berry

*A production of Mr. Burbank's which shows how,
by crossing plants out of kind, we are helping them to start new
species which will be free from inherited disadvantages,
and bear us, bountifully, better crops.*

LUTHER BURBANK

"Poor man! Whatever may have been thought of his good taste, or his tact, or his judgment, I could hardly take offense at his sentiments—for they really reflected the thought of that day.

"Poor man! He could not see that our plants are what they are because they have grown up with the birds, and the bees, and the winds to help them; and that now, after all these centuries of uphill struggle, man has been given to them as a partner to free them from weakness and open new doors of opportunity.

"He could not see that all of us, the birds, and the bees, and the flowers, and we, ourselves, are a part of the same onward-moving procession, each helping the other to better things; nor could many of the others of his time see that.

"And the botanists of that day, less than four short decades ago, found their chief work in the study and classification of dried and shriveled plant mummies, whose souls had fled—rather than in the living, breathing forms, anxious to reveal their life histories.

"They counted the stamens of a dried flower without looking at the causes for those stamens; they measured and surveyed the length and breadth of truth with never a thought of its depth—they charted its surface, as if never realizing that it was a thing of three dimensions.

ON FACT VS. THEORY

"And that is why those who had devoted their lifetimes to counting stamens and classifying shapes told me, through their writings, that a cross might be made within species, but never between species; that is why when I did make a cross between species they looked no further into the truth, but simply moved up a notch, and said, 'Very well, but you cannot make a cross between genera'; that is why, when I did that very thing, not once, but scores of times, that type of scientist lost interest in rule making and went back to stamen counting."

* * * * * *

To realize the point more clearly, let us observe for a moment the common tomato—which belongs to that large division of plants, the nightshade family.

Just as the rose family includes not only the rose, but the apple and the blackberry and sixty-two other plants, so the nightshade family includes seventy-five genera and more than eighteen hundred species.

The classification is built around structural facts, such as that plants of this family originally had alternate leaves with five stamens and a two-celled ovary, or egg chamber, each cell containing many eggs.

These structural similarities in the plants of

[229]

Improved Tigridias

This South American plant with which Mr. Burbank has experimented now bears blossoms six or seven inches in diameter, of wonderful formation and color and with striking tiger spots which add to the weird beauty of the flower.

this family trace back to a common parentage and fully justify the classification of these seventy-five genera in a single family.

If we were to look not at the structure, however, but at the seventy-five plants themselves, then, and only then, could we fully realize the wonders which environment, toying with that common heredity within the plant, has wrought.

We should see, among the seventy-five brothers and sisters of that family if they were spread before us, the poisonous bitter-sweet, and the humble but indispensable potato; the egg plant and the Jerusalem cherry; the horse nettle and the jimson weed; the tobacco plant and the beautiful petunia; and the tomato itself.

We should see seventy-five plants with original structural similarities, yet differing, in every other way, as night differs from day; and we should be able to trace, if we observed closely enough, the points at which, in the history of this family, new environment, oft repeated, has hardened into heredity, subject to the call of still newer environment, which has not been lacking to bring it out; we should be able to trace out, by easy stages, why one branch ran to the poisonous bitter-sweet, another to the potato with its food product below the ground, another to the tomato with its tempting fruit displayed on vines above; another

[231]

to tobacco, valued for its chemical content—and so on throughout all of the variations.

The tomato, we should see, was the last of the family to fall into a violent change of environment.

A tropical plant, bearing fruits about the size of a hickory nut and not believed to be edible, the tomato found its way into the United States within the past century.

At first, the tomato plant was prized merely as an ornament; it was grown as we now grow rose bushes, and the fruit was looked upon as a mantel decoration, until, by accident, it was discovered to be edible. There are, in fact, many such ornamentals today which might bear us edible fruit. One, in particular, the passion flower, which Mr. Burbank is developing, will form the subject of an interesting description later on.

Following the discovery that the tomato was edible came the same course of unconscious selection that falls to the lot of every useful plant. The biggest tomatoes were saved, the better tomatoes were cultivated.

In the environment of the tropics, the tomato fruit of hickory nut size was ideal; it cost less effort to produce than a larger tomato; it contained sufficient seeds to insure reproduction.

But with the advent of man into its environment, its seed cham' ers increased in number, the

Variable Potato Seedlings

While the tomato has been so thoroughly fixed in a few decades that many varieties reproduce true to seed, its cousin, the potato, as explained in Chapter II, runs into wonderful variations when its seed is planted. The potato seedlings pictured here are some which were grown from the seed in the potato seed balls shown on page 57.

meat surrounding the seeds increased in quantity and improved in quality; so that in virtually half a century the large, luscious, juicy tomato we now know is universally to be found in our markets, in season and out.

No man can say how many thousands or tens of thousands of years it took wild environment to separate the tomato from the seventy-four others of its family. Yet, in less than half a century, see what changes man, as an element of environment, has worked!

We take the seeds of our *Ponderosa* tomatoes and set them out in a can or a shallow box, and midsummer brings us new *Ponderosas*—so well have we succeeded in fixing the traits we desire.

But were we to take those same seeds to the tropics and plant them under the conditions of only fifty years ago an entirely different thing would happen.

The first generation would be *Ponderosas*, more or less like those we grow here.

But in the second generation, or, at latest, the third, the seeds of those very *Ponderosas*, when planted, would grow into vines which bear the old type of tomato—the size of a hickory nut—an immediate response, almost, to the wild tropical environment which prevailed before man came along.

[234]

ON FACT VS. THEORY

From the botanists of only a century ago, examining only dead tomato blossoms from the tropics, and dried tomato fruits the size of hickory nuts—how could we expect an inkling, even, of what the tomato with less than half a century of cultivation could become?

How short, indeed, the time which environment requires to transform a plant beyond recognition —especially when man, either consciously or unconsciously, becomes a part of that environment!

And, knowing what the Chinese did to the pear, what the American Indian did to corn, what our own fathers and mothers did to the tomato, can we not see that, while stamen counting has its place, yet, for real achievements in plant improvement, we must look for help not so much to the stamen counters as to the plants themselves as new environment brings their old heredities into view.

* * * * *

Mr. Burbank has made combinations between species; he has made combinations between genera, not once, but many times; fertile, seed-bearing combinations.

How far, then, can plant combination be carried? Is it possible to go above the genus and make combinations between families? Or to go above the family and make combinations between the orders? Or to go above the orders and make

Some Blackberry Canes

It is possible, from the appearance of the cane of the blackberry, at certain stages, to predict the color of the fruit which is later to be borne. The application of this short-cut is fully explained under a later heading. The picture above shows a range of variation produced by crossing.

combinations between the classes? Or to go above the classes and make combinations between the subkingdoms?

"Give us time," says Mr. Burbank, "and we could accomplish anything.

"The limitations of our work are not limitations imposed by Nature; they are limitations imposed, alone, by the clock and the calendar.

"Here we are, fighting ten thousand years of hardened heredity with five or ten years of new environment; sometimes we succeed; it is no wonder that more often we fail; in five years, however, we can usually work a transformation; if we could afford to spend fifty years on a single plant, we could upset every rule that has ever been formulated about that plant; and if we could spend five thousand years, we could, simply by guiding Nature, accomplish, well, *anything*.

"Every season we are working changes which Nature would take ages to work; but from a practical standpoint we must seek always to take advantage of the old heredities which Nature has stored up—to make them serve our ends, because this can be done quickly; rather than to create and fix new heredities which might take so long as to rob our work of its usefulness."

* * * * *

Here, then, is Mr. Burbank's bird's-eye view:

[237]

Before us is a world of living, onward-marching plants—plants which have made, are making, and will continue to make, their own rules as they go along. Here, before us, too, is the propaganda of our subject with its maps, plans, charts, rules, laws, theories, beliefs, built up too fixedly, too arbitrarily, too superficially, perhaps, but very completely, nevertheless, around this onward-marching mass.

Let us use to the utmost all the help that science can give; to save time, let us accept the laws and the rules, let us have confidence in the maps and the charts, until the *plants themselves* show our error.

Let us search, always, for stored up heredities to convert to our use, just as we would seek stored up diamonds, or gold, or coal, instead of trying, by chemistry, to produce them.

Let us realize, always, that everything is possible with time; but let us seek out all the short-cuts we can.

For, after all, we have so little of Time!

*　　*　　*　　*　　*

With time as our limiting factor, then, we shall find, in plant work, many things which we cannot hope to accomplish.

We shall find plants, of course, of different species, and different genera—a surprising num-

[238]

A Typical
Burbank Plum

The direct color
photograph print shown
here represents one of several hundred new plums
produced by Mr. Burbank
during the summer of 1913.
Not all of these plums by
any means are improve-
ments, but out of the
number, possibly two or
three may be propagated
for introduction. The luscious plum shown here
has as yet received
no name.

ber, in spite of the old belief, which will combine readily to produce fertile offspring constituting a new species or a new genus.

We shall find plants of different species or genera which combine to make a sterile offspring —a mule among plants.

And we shall find plants which can hardly be combined at all—plants in which the pollen of one seems to act as a definite poison on the other— plants with large pollen grains which cannot push their tubes down the pistils of smaller flowers— and plants which, through long fixed heredity, seem as averse to combination as oil seems averse to combining with water.

"But no man," says Mr. Burbank, who has just read this, "can tell until he has tried—tried not once, but thousands and thousands of times."

*   *   *   *   *

"What is that?" asked a seedsman who was visiting Mr. Burbank.

"That is a *Nicotunia*," replied Mr. Burbank, "and you are the first man in the world who has ever seen one. It is the name which I have given to a new race of plants produced by crossing the large flowering *nicotianas*, or tobacco plants, with petunias. It is, as you can see, a cross between two genera of the nightshade family."

"H'm!" said the seedsman.

[240]

ON FACT VS. THEORY

"You know the secret now," said Mr. Burbank, "but if you think that you can produce these *nico-tunias* as you would hybrid petunias, or crossbred primroses, go ahead and try; there is no patent on their manufacture; but if the five hundredth cross succeeds, or even the five thousandth, under the best conditions obtainable, you will surely be very successful. I do not fear any immediate competition. This one cost me ten thousand tries."

Perhaps those who have said that species could not be combined with species, or genus with genus have tried only once or twice or a dozen times. Perhaps Mr. Burbank's patience and persistence account for some of the upset laws.

* * * * *

"Why not content ourselves to work within varieties as the bees work?" asks some one.

"Because by going out of the varieties and combining between species, and going out of the species and combining between genera, we multiply almost infinitely the combinations of old heredities which we may bring into play—we lessen the work which we have to make environment do by spreading before us more combinations of heredity—we accomplish in two years what otherwise might take two lifetimes."

In all, Mr. Burbank has made one hundred and seventy-nine combinations between different

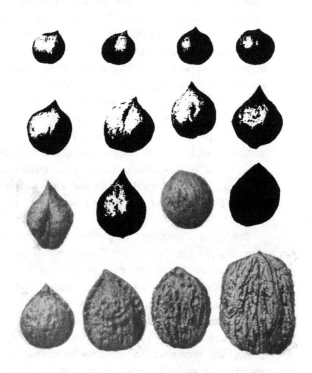

Variations in Walnuts

*All of the variations pictured above were secured by crossing.
Mr. Burbank, in his walnut work, has grown nuts by the wagon load
for the purpose of finding one or two which came near his ideal.*

species and different genera, treated elsewhere, all of which were thought to be impossible.

It was such combinations as these which enabled him to perfect the cactus, to produce the plumcot, to make the Shasta daisy—in fact, it was Luther Burbank's lack of respect for man-made laws, when plants told him a different story, that has given the world eighty per cent. of his productions—that has led him to ninety per cent. of his discoveries in practical method.

"The only reason," said Mr. Burbank, "that we do not combine between families, and between orders, and classes, is that we haven't the time."

* * * * *

So we see that the science of plant life is not an exact science, like mathematics, in which two and two always equal four. It is not a science in which the definite answers to specific problems can be found in the back of any book.

It is a science which involves endless experimenting—endless seeking after better and better results.

Theories are good, because, if we do not permit them to mislead us, they may save us time; laws, and maps, and charts, and diagrams—systems of classification and of nomenclature—all these are good, because, if they are faulty, they still reveal to us the viewpoint of som on who, with liligence, has devoted himself to a single phase, at least, of a complex subject.

But we must remember that the theories, most of them, are built around *dead* plants.

While the facts we are to use are to be gathered from *living* ones.

So, every once in a while, when we come to a crossroads where that kind of theory and this kind of fact seem to part, let us stick to the thing which the living plant tells us, and assume that evolution, or improvement, or progress, or whatever we choose to call it, has stolen another lap on the plant historians.

And let us remember that the fact that ours is not an exact science, with fixed answers to its problems, is more than made up for by the compensating fact that there seems to be no limit to the perfection to which plant achievements may be carried—no impassable barrier, apparently (save time—which limits us all, in everything), beyond which our experiments may not go.

> *—Nature did not make the laws; she limits herself to no grooves; she travels to no set schedule.*

Some Plants Which Are Begging for Immediate Improvement

A Rough Survey of
the Possibilities

I HAVE finished making an analysis of a number of your fruits," wrote a chemist to Mr. Burbank, "and I find that pectic acid, which is so apt to play havoc with the human digestive tract, and which accounts for the inability of many people to enjoy raw fruit, is almost entirely absent."

"It must be, then, that I don't like pectic acid," commented Mr. Burbank as he read the letter.

"It never occurred to me to give the matter of its elimination a thought; so, the only way I can account for the lack of it is that, as I have selected my fruits by tasting, I have preferred those which were low in this content."

*   *   *   *   *

It would be no small achievement to rebuild our fruits and grains and vegetables to fit the finnicky stomachs which sedentary occupations are giving us. Yet such a transformation is one which might be easily wrought in a few years through simple selection, and serves, here, to illustrate the vast range of possibilities in plant improvement which only wait willing hands and active minds to turn them into realization.

Immediate possibilities for plant improvement, indeed, outnumber the improvements which have already been wrought, ten thousand to one.

It is planned in these books to treat of the possibilities of each plant separately, in connection with the description of the work which has already been done, since each of Mr. Burbank's improvements not only suggests countless other improvements which he has not had the time to take up, but indicates, in a measure, the method by which their accomplishment may be brought about.

It may be well, at this point, however, to survey, roughly, the range of possibilities for improvement, so that, as we go along, we may have an appreciative eye for the value of the things which are clamoring to be done.

*   *   *   *   *

The incident of the pectic acid is but one of many unexpected improvements which Mr. Burbank has discovered in his productions after his first object has been achieved.

ON THE POSSIBILITIES

Possibly as striking an illustration of this as could be chosen is one which made itself evident in the plumcot.

So intent was Mr. Burbank on his purpose of combining two species, the plum and the apricot— so single-minded was his idea of producing a fruit which should reflect its double parentage in flesh and flavor—that he lost sight of some of the incidental possibilities of such a combination.

The cross having been made, however, he set about to study the other new characters which the combination showed.

Some of these were recognized as being of little practical value.

The foliage of the plumcot tree, for example, does not necessarily resemble the plum or the apricot, being intermediate and representing a perfect blend. Though, it may be noted in passing, the foliage of a cross or hybrid often takes on the characteristics of either one parent or the other, or may consist of varicolored leaves, or may even present leaves of two distinct kinds. This is an interesting and important subject which will be clearly illustrated with direct color photographs later.

Finding the plumcot foliage a blend, Mr. Burbank was not surprised to discover that the root of the plumcot tree resembled in color neither the bright red of the apricot, nor the pale yellow of the plum, but was of an intermediate shade.

Of the thousands of characteristics of the parent species as they were subjected to examination and analysis, the most startling was found in the surface texture of the fruit itself—one of the most novel effects, in fact, to be seen in all Nature.

The apricot has a fine velvety skin which serves not only as a protection to the fruit from insects and from the sun's withering rays, but which adds greatly to its attractive appearance.

Plums, usually, are overspread with a delicate white or bluish bloom, powdery in form, easily defaced by the slightest handling. This bloom adds a touch of delicacy and beauty to the fruit, suggests its freshness, and intensifies the attractiveness of the colors underneath.

In the early plumcots it was noticed that many had a softer, more velvety skin than the apricot, and that this persisted after much handling. Then, as the characteristics began to settle, after several generations of plumcots had appeared, it was noticed that the new fruit not only had the attractive velvety skin of the apricot, but that this velvet overspread and protected a bloom like that of the plum, giving the plumcot the plum's delicacy of appearance, with the apricot's hardiness to handling.

Perishable Bloom

From this direct color photograph print the result of handling plums may be imagined. These plums have been defaced merely by the swishing of the branches of the tree on which they grew. Since the bloom suggests the freshness of the fruit, its perishability is a great drawback in handling and shipping plums to the market.

When this blend of bloom and velvet was noted, experiments were made to determine how much handling it would withstand. A dozen plumcots were passed around from hand to hand possibly hundreds of times, and then left to decay, the condition of the velvet bloom being noted from time to time.

While there was a slight decrease in the brilliancy of the bloom, yet it persisted to a surprising degree even after the flesh of the plumcot had decayed.

The accompanying color photograph prints show clearly the difference in appearance between the plum and the plumcot after being subjected to handling.

The value of this characteristic is greater than might first be estimated. Plums lose their bloom to a great extent, even on the tree—by brushing of leaves or chafing together. Wherever foliage or other fruit touches it, the bloom is injured or destroyed beyond repair. It is of course impossible to get the plum to market without rubbing off the greater part of the bloom and giving the fruit a mussy appearance. In making the photographs in these books, in fact, it has been found difficult, first to find the fruit which has a perfect bloom on the tree; and second, to get the plum in front of the camera without defacing it.

[250]

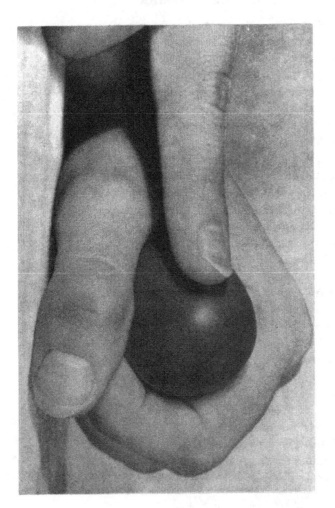

The plumcot inher-
ited part of the fuzz
of its parent apricot, together with the beautiful
bloom of its plum parent—
with the result that the
fuzz protects the bloom and
makes it practically indestructible. In this photograph print the finger had
been drawn heavily
across the fruit,
but no mark
was left.

Wherever a finger touches the plum a mark is left, and since fruits, at best, must receive much handling from the orchard to the ultimate consumer, the plum is likely to lose its charm long before its real freshness or flavor has begun to depreciate.

With the plumcots, however, the velvety bloom remains through growing, picking, sorting, shipping, handling and sale. Which means, of course, that the grower, the shipper, and the dealer receive a better profit, and the consumer pays the extra cost with cheerfulness, because appearance, after all, is nearly as valuable a point in a fruit as size, flavor or sweetness.

This one, unplanned, unexpected improvement in the plumcot increases the earning capacity of the fruit by more than $100.00 per acre over what could be earned if plumcots had an evanescent bloom like their parent plums.

Which is simply another evidence of the importance, in plant improvement (and elsewhere) of things which, at first, we are too apt to regard as trifles.

It is the seeming trifles, after all, which appear to have the greatest effect on prices and profits. Of the two tins of asparagus shown here, one commands more than twice the retail price of the other, and brings considerably more than double

Both Good Asparagus

*This direct color photograph print shows the advantage
of selecting asparagus for durability as well as for size and
flavor. One tin shows stalks which are whole and tempting—the
other stalks which, during the process of cooking and canning, have broken and become messy. The unbroken
asparagus costs no more to raise but commands twice as great a market price.*

the profit to the asparagus grower, simply because of the trifle that the more costly asparagus stands up through all the operations from the garden to the table, while the other, broken down in structure, presents a messy, unappetizing appearance when served.

Since it costs no more to raise the higher priced asparagus, after the expense of a few seasons of selection has been paid for, what excuse can there be for producing the other kind?

It would be impossible, here, to begin to catalog the improvements which can be wrought—improvements in the size, shape, color, texture, juiciness, flavor, sweetness, or chemical content of fruits; improvements in the appearance, tenderness, taste, cooking qualities, and nutritive elements in vegetables; improvements in length and strength of fiber in cotton, flax and hemp; improvements in size, flavor, solidity, thinness of shell of nuts; improvements in the quantity and the quality of kernels in grains; improvements in amount and in value of the chemical content of sugar beets, sorghum, coffee, tea and all other plants which are raised for their extracts; improvements, wonderful improvements, in the stalk of corn, even, so that though we could make it bear no more kernels, or no more ears, it would still yield us a better and bigger forage crop;

improvements, all of them, which are capable of turning losses into profits, and of multiplying profits, instead of merely adding to them by single per cents.

* * * * *

Improving the yield and, consequently, the usefulness and profit of existing plants, however, is but the beginning of the work before us.

An almost equally rich field lies in saving plants from their own extravagance, thereby increasing the yield.

The fruit trees of our fathers and mothers were shade trees in size, with all too little fruit.

The ideal orchard of today, generally speaking, is the one which can be picked without the use of a step ladder. Thus, already, we have taught fruit bearing plants economy—saved them the extravagance of making unnecessary wood, at the expense of fruit, since it is their fruit, not their wood, that we want.

The grapes of our childhood grew sparsely on climbing vines which covered our arbors; while the grapes grown for profit today grow thickly, almost solidly, on stubby plants three feet or so in height. The value of the grape plant lies in the fruit and not in the vine.

In so many different ways can we save our plants extravagance and increase their useful

[255]

Transforming the Gladiolus

When Mr. Burbank first began his work with the gladiolus,
its blossoms were widely separated on a long stalk.   The direct
color photograph print above shows how he has brought them into a
compact mass, and how, in many cases, he has trained them
to bloom around the entire stalk instead of only on two
sides as before.   Mr. Burbank also increased the
size and strength of the gladiolus stalk that
it might better withstand the winds—
all of these things in addition
to the wonderful improve-
ments he has wrought
in the flower itself.

products by curbing their useless ones, that it would not be possible to list them here.

But, aside from these, and in the same category, there are countless other new improvements to be wrought.

The stoneless plum points the way to a new world of fruits in which the stony or shell-like covering of the seeds has been bred away.

The coreless apple, pear and quince, with sheathless seeds growing compactly near the top, out of the way—these are all within the range of accomplishment.

Seedless raspberries, blackberries, gooseberries, currants, with the energy saved reinvested in added size or better flavor, call for some one to bring them about. Seedless grapes we have had for more than a century; yet by a certain cross which Mr. Burbank will suggest in the grape chapter, he believes that they can be doubled in size and much improved in flavor. Seedless figs, even, might be made, but these could be counted no improvement; for the seeds of the fig give the fruit its flavor.

Seedless watermelons might mean more work than the result would repay, but navel watermelons, with seeds arranged as in the navel orange, would, likely enough, yield a result commensurate with the effort required to produce them.

[257]

LUTHER BURBANK

Thornless blackberries and spineless cactus are productions of proven worth and long standing, which Mr. Burbank has now followed up with his thornless raspberry—with many other thornless plants to come. Why thorns at all, in the world of useful plants, when useful plants no longer need them?

Whatever plant we observe we shall see some waste which might be eliminated, some weakness which might be overcome, some extravagance which might be checked—and all for the profit of producer and consumer alike.

* * * * *

Still another important department of plant improvement lies in fitting plants to meet specific conditions.

The grape growers of California, for example, had their vineyards destroyed by a little plant louse called the phylloxera, a pest which not only attacks the leaves, but the roots as well, and kills the vine. The growers found relief through grafting new vines on resistant roots which environment had armored against this pest.

When we think of the cactus, and the sage-brush, and the desert euphorbia—of the conditions which, unaided, they have withstood and the enemies which they have overcome, does it not seem as if, with our help, we should be able to

[258]

A New Thornless Fruit

*Mr. Burbank's thornless blackberry is well known, and
now, by the application of the same methods, he has produced
his first thornless raspberry. Plants which are under cultivation no
longer have need for thorns and it is possible to save them
the extravagance of producing them so that they may
have more energy to put into their useful product.*

An Apple Chunky

This direct color photograph print shows the result of the work of the larva of the codling moth. There are several measures which can be adopted to keep this pest out of the orchard—but is it not possible to produce a new apple which shall be resistant to this enemy, as certain grapes are now resistant to the phylloxera?

produce new races of plants to withstand the boll weevil, the codling moth and the San Jose scale; and with complaints so broadcast, and successes so marked and so many, does not the perfection of disease- and pest-resisting varieties seem an important and lucrative field?

Nor are the insects and diseases the only enemies which plants can be taught to overcome. Mr. Burbank has trained trees to bloom later in the season so as to avoid the late frosts which might nip the buds; and to bear earlier, that their fruit may be gathered before the early frosts of fall have come to destroy. He has encouraged the gladiolus to thicken its stalk and to rearrange its blossoms, so that the wind no longer ruins its beauty.

And the prune, which must lie on the ground till it cures, had the habit, here in California, of ripening at about the time of the equinoctial rains of fall. Mr. Burbank helped it to shift its bearing season earlier so that, now, when the rains come, the prune crop has been harvested and is safely under cover.

In all of these enemies of plant life, the insects, and the diseases, and the rains, and the frosts, and the snows, and even the parching heat of the plains, there are opportunities for the plant improver.

[261]

Yet these enemies form the least important, perhaps, of the special conditions to which plants may be accommodated.

The market demand, for example, is a specific condition which well repays any effort expended in transforming plants to meet it.

The early cherries, and the early asparagus, and the early corn—and every fruit and food which can be offered before the heavy season opens, is rewarded with a fancy price which means a fancy profit to its producer.

The early bearers, too, may be supplanted with those still earlier, until the extra early ones overlap the extra late ones. Mr. Burbank now has strawberries, which, in climates where there is no frost severe enough to prevent, bear the year around.

Mr. Burbank's winter rhubarb, another year-around bearer, as well as his plumcot with its indestructible bloom, are improvements which show what can be done in the way of meeting market demand.

His cherries, which have retailed at $3.10 a pound because of their lusciousness and their earliness, give an idea of the profit of changing the bearing periods of our plants as against taking their output as it comes.

Beside the market demand for fresh fruits

and vegetables ahead of time, there is an almost equally great demand, later on in the season, from the canners.

The illustration of the asparagus which stands canning as against equally good asparagus which does not, typifies the needs of this demand. The same truth applies to tree fruits and berries and vegetables—to everything that undergoes the preserving process.

Some plants are more profitable when their bearing season is lengthened as much as possible; some, as has been seen, when it is made earlier or later; but Mr. Burbank faced a different condition when he produced his Empson pea.

The canners wanted a very small green pea to imitate the French one which is so much used. Quite a little problem in chemistry was involved. Peas half grown are two-thirds sweeter than peas full grown, because, toward the end, their sugar begins to go a step further and turn into starch. With these demands in mind, Mr. Burbank planted and selected, and planted and selected until he had the qualities he wanted in a pea of the right size when it was half ripe.

But still another element entered—peas for canning should ripen all at one time and not straggle out over a week or two. The reason for this being that, if they ripen all at once, they may be harvested by machinery so that the cost of handling is cut to the minimum.

Mr. Burbank took the peas which he had selected for form, size, color, taste, content, and productiveness; then picked them over and, out of tens of thousands, got perhaps one or two hundred peas which he planted separately. These, then, he harvested by separately counting the pods and counting the peas, until he had finally combined in his selection not only the best of the lot but those which ripened at the same time—practically on the same day. Today those Burbank Empson peas form the chief industry of a large community.

There are countless other requirements which can be equally well met—countless little economies which can be taught to the plants—little, as applied to any specific plant, but tremendous in the aggregate.

There is, for instance, Mr. Burbank's new canning cherry which, when picked, leaves its stone on the tree. It would seem a small thing to one eating the cherries as he picks them off the. tree. Yet, think of the saving, as carload after carload of these are brought to the cannery—the saving at a time when minutes count, when help is short, generally, and when the fruit, because of heat, is in danger of spoiling—under these

Leaves the Stone on the Tree

This direct color photograph print shows one of Mr. Burbank's new productions, a canning cherry which, when picked, leaves the pit on the tree. The saving in not having to pit the cherries at the canning factory although, at first apparently trifling, is, in the aggregate, larger than would be supposed; particularly in view of the fact that the canning seasons are so short that much fruit spoils through handling and through the delay which handling necessitates.

conditions think of the saving in not having to pit them.

The list could be extended almost endlessly, from thickening the skin of the plum so as to enable it to be shipped to South Africa and back, as Mr. Burbank has done, to the production of a tomato, which, when placed in boiling water, will shed its skin without peeling—which Mr. Burbank says can be done.

Under the head of saving a plant from its own extravagance might well come the large subject of bringing trees to early fruiting, or of shortening the period from seed to maturity in shade and lumber trees. Mr. Burbank's quick growing walnut, and his pineapple quince and chestnut seedlings bearing crops at six months, stand forth as strong encouragement to those who would take up this line.

Then, too, under the same heading of fitting plants to meet new conditions, whole chapters might be written on how the fig tree could be adapted to New England; or how Minnesota might be made one of the greatest fruit producing states, or how almost any plant might, in time, be adapted to any soil or any climate.

And, conversely, there is the broad subject of adapting plants to special localities. The hop crop of Sonoma County, California, the cabbage crop near Racine, Wisconsin, the celery crop near Kalamazoo, the canteloupe crop at Rocky Ford— all of these bear eloquent testimony to the profit of a specialty properly introduced.

Who can say how many who are making only a hand-to-mouth living out of corn or wheat, simply because they are in corn or wheat countries, could not fit some special plant to their worn out soil?

And who, seeing that some forms of plant life not only exist, but thrive, under the most adverse conditions, shall say that there is any poor land, anywhere? Is it not the fact that poor land usually means that the plants have been poorly chosen for it, or poorly adapted to it?

These are all problems which will be treated in their proper places, problems which offer rich rewards to plant improvers of determination and patience.

*　*　*　*　*

So far, in these opportunities for plant improvement, we have referred only to the betterment of plants now under cultivation.

When we remember that every useful plant which now grows to serve us was once a wild plant, and when we begin to check over the list of those wild plants which have not yet been improved, the possibilities are almost staggering.

[267]

A Wild Plant Improved

This direct color photograph print shows the wild New England aster and the improvement which a single season of selection by Mr. Burbank worked. All of our cultivated plants came from the wild, but the possibility of improving wild plants, so far from being exhausted, has, in fact, only been touched.

ON THE POSSIBILITIES

Not all plants, of course, are worth working with—not all have within them heredities which could profitably be brought forth. But as a safe comparison, it might be stated that the proportion between present useful plants and those in the wild which can be made useful, is at least as great or greater than the proportion between the coal which has already been mined, and the coal which is stored up for us in the ground. Greater, by probably a hundred times, for while we have depleted our coal supply, our plants have been multiplying, not only in number, but in kind and in form.

Moreover, from our wild plants, we may not only get new products, but new strength, new hardiness, new combative powers, and endless other desirable new qualities for our tame plants.

All of these things are just as immediate as possibilities, as transcontinental railroads were fifty years ago. All of these things can be made to come about with such apparent ease that future generations will take them as a matter of course.

Yet we have not touched, so far, on the most interesting field in plant improvement — the production, through crossing, hybridizing and selection, of entirely new plants to meet entirely new demands.

Who shall produce some plant—and there are

Improving the Sunflower

Even the common sunflower has possibilities for improvement as a useful plant. Sunflower seed is greatly prized by poultry raisers for feed. But the improvements which Mr. Burbank is working, along different lines which will be described later, may transform this into one of the most useful of plants.

plenty of suggestions toward this end—which shall utilize cheap land to give the world its supply of wood pulp for paper making, the demand for which has already eaten up our forests and is fast encroaching on Canada's?

Who shall say that within twenty years there will not be some new plant better than flax, some plant which, unlike flax for this purpose, can be grown in the United States, to supply us with a fabric as cheap as cotton, but as fine as linen?

Who will be the one to produce a plant which shall yield us rubber—a plant growing, perhaps, on the deserts, which shall make the cost of motor car tires seem only an insignificant item in upkeep?

And who, on those same deserts, and growing, perhaps, side by side, shall perfect a plant which can be transformed into five cent alcohol for the motors themselves?

*　*　*　*　*

We see that the openings for plant improvement broadly divide themselves into four classes.

First, improving the quality of the product of existing plants.

Second, saving plants from their own extravagance, thereby increasing their yield.

Third, fitting plants more closely to specific conditions of soil, climate and locality.

Most of nature's trunks and stems are round, but the stalk of this particular kind of sunflower is undeniably square—and with a square hole inside. The leaves, it will be noted, form a cup around the stalk which fill with water to quench the thirst of the plant. Since square stalks are possible, is it not within reason to believe that fruits may be produced which, if not exactly cubical will, at least pack more economically than spherical fruits? Some of Mr. Burbank's plum improvements have been along this line.

ON THE POSSIBILITIES

And fourth, transforming wild plants and making entirely new ones to take care of new wants which are growing with surprising rapidity.

*　　*　　*　　*　　*

The cost and quality of everything that we eat and wear depend on this work of plant improvement.

The beefsteak for which we are paying an ever-increasing price represents, after all, so many blades of grass or, perhaps, so many slabs of cactus; while the potatoes, the lettuce and the coffee which go with it come out of the ground direct.

Our shirts are from cotton or flax, or from the mulberry tree on which the silkworm feeds.

Our shoes, like our steaks, resolve themselves into grass; while our woolen coats represent the grass which the sheep found after the cows got through.

The mineral kingdom supplies the least of our needs; and the animal kingdom feeds on, and depends on, the vegetable kingdom, after all.

*　　*　　*　　*　　*

"Who can predict the result," asks Mr. Burbank, "when the inventive genius of young America is turned toward this, the greatest of all fields of invention, as it is now turned towai i mechanics and electricity?"

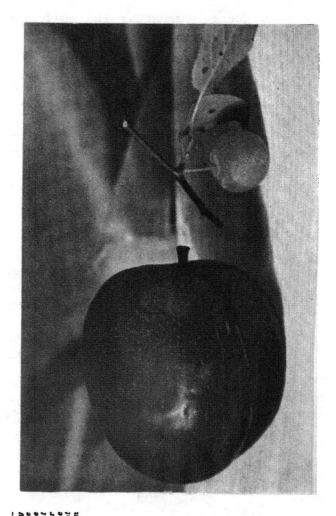

Ancestor

When plants grow wild there is little need for large quantities of luscious meat; but as they come under cultivation the stone grows less and the meat not only more but better. This direct color photograph print is of one of Mr. Burbank's latest plums and of a wild plum such as grows in the woods near Santa Rosa; both are actual size.

Piecing the Fragments
of a
Motion Picture Film

We Stop to Take
A Backward Glance

WHEN you speak of environment as an active influence," Mr. Burbank was asked, "do you mean the soil and the rainfall and the climate?"

"Yes," was the reply. "I mean those; but not only those; I mean, too, such elements of environment as the Union Pacific Railroad.

* * * * *

"I will explain," Mr. Burbank continued.

"Go out into the woods, almost anywhere in the United States, and hunt up a wild plum tree, and you will find that it bears a poor little fruit with a great big stone.

"You see, the only purpose which the wild plum has in surrounding its seed with a fruit is to attract the animals so that they may carry it away from the foot of the parent tree and plant it in

[VOLUME I—CHAPTER IX]

new surroundings, for the good of the offspring and the race. It takes very little meat, and very little in the way of attractive appearance to accomplish this purpose; and besides, the wild plum has to put so much of its vitality into stone, in order to protect the seed within it from the sharp teeth of the same animals which carry it away, that it has little energy left to devote to beauty and flavor.

"Then take the same wild plum after it has been brought under cultivation and as it grows in the average backyard, and you will find a transformation — less stone, more meat, better flavor, finer aroma, more regular shape, brighter color.

"This, however, represents but the first stage in the progress of the plum; with all this improvement the backyard plum still may not be useful for any commercial purpose; because people with plum trees in their backyards are likely to eat the fruit off the tree, or to give it to their neighbors, or to cook and preserve it as soon as ripe. So, even the cultivated backyard plum may be perfectly satisfactory for its purpose without having those keeping qualities necessary in a commercial fruit.

"And this is the point at which the Union Pacific Railroad entered into its environment—at least into the environment of the California plum.

"The railroad became a factor in plum improvement by bringing millions of plum-hungry easterners within reach—by affording quick and economical shipping facilities where there had been no shipping facilities at all before.

"Much as the time of transcontinental travel was reduced, the backyard plum could not withstand the journey. But with an eager market as an incentive, made possible through the railroad, people began to select plums for shipment, until the plum graduated from its backyard environment and became the basis of a thriving industry. The railroad, by bringing customers within reach of those who had plums which would stand shipment, and charging as much to ship poor plums as good plums, encouraged selection not only for shipping plums, but toward a better and better quality of fruit which, without doubt, in the absence of the market which the railroad provided, would never have been produced.

"Thus we see three important stages in the transformation of the plum.

"First, the wild era.

"Second, the backyard era.

"Third, the railroad era."

*   *   *   *   *

When we stop to think of it, all of the great

improvements in plant life have been wrought in
the railroad era—using the railroad, figuratively,
to represent all of the invention, wealth and
progress which have accompanied it.

There are, after all, but one hundred and forty
generations between us and Adam, if the popular
notions of elapsed time are correct—but one
hundred and forty father-to-son steps between
the Garden of Eden and now—but one hundred
and forty lifetimes, all told, in which whatever
progress we have made has been accomplished.

Yet our plants go back, who knows how many
tens of thousands of generations?

It took the plum tree all of these uncounted
ages, in which it had only wild environment, to
produce the poor little fruit which we find growing
in the woods.

It took only two or three short centuries of
care and half-hearted selection to bring about the
improvement which is evidenced in the common
backyard plum.

And it took less than a generation, after the
railroads came, to work all of the real wonders
which we see in this fruit today.

The last two generations of the human race,
in fact, have accomplished more toward real
progress—have done more to make transportation
and quick communication possible—have gone

further in invention, art, science, and general
knowledge—than the one hundred and thirty-eight
generations, which preceded them, combined.

So, up to two or three human generations ago,
the plants, with their start of tens of thousands
of generations, were abreast of or ahead of human
needs.

But human inventive genius, going ahead
hundreds or thousands of years at a jump,
bringing with it organization and specialization,
has changed all of that.

In our race across the untracked plains before
us, we have outrun our plants. That is all. And,
having outrun them, we must lend a hand to
bring them up with us if they are to meet our
requirements.

* * * * *

Shall we content ourselves with watering our
plants when they are dry; and enriching the soil
when it is worn out; shall we be satisfied merely
to be good gardeners?

Or shall we study the living forces within the
plants themselves and let them teach us how to
work real transformations?

* * * * *

It is conceivable that a manufacturer · of
machinery might become successful, or even rise
to be the foremost manufacturer in his line,

without giving a moment of consideration to the atom-structure of the iron which he works—with never a thought of the forces which Nature has employed in creating the substance we call iron ore.

It is conceivable that one might become a good cook—a master chef, even—without the slightest reference to, or knowledge of, the structural formation of animal cells and vegetable cells.

Or that one might succeed as a teacher of the young—might become, even, a nation-wide authority on molding the plastic mind of youth—without ever being assailed by the thought that the forbears of the nimble-minded children in his care, ages and ages ago, may have been swinging from tree to tree by their tails.

And so, in most occupations, it has been contrived for us that we deal only with present-day facts and conditions—that there is little incentive, aside from general interest or wandering curiosity, to try to lift the veil which obscures our past—or to peer through the fog which keeps us from seeing what tomorrow has in store.

In plant growing, more than in any of the world's other industries, does the scheme of evolution and a working knowledge of Nature's methods cease to be a theory — of far-away importance and of no immediate interest—and

Snow-on-the-Mountain

This odd plant is shown here to illustrate the necessity of studying not merely the form of a plant but the forces within it. It receives its name because when it blooms its leaves begin to turn white. The purpose of this, Mr. Burbank says, is to help guide the insects to the blossom in order to insure reproduction. It will be noted that the leaves which do not lead to blossoms remain green, while those which surround the blossoms form brilliantly illumined pathways for the insects. Few plants give outward evidences of their processes so clearly as this—but the forces of heredity and environment are there—none the less —and it is these forces which we must study if we are to help plants to improvement.

become an actual working factor, a necessary tool, without which it is impossible to do the day's work.

Whether plant improvement be taken up as a science, or as a profession, or as a business—or whether it be considered merely a thing of general interest, an idle hour recreation—there is ever present the need to understand Nature's methods and her forces in order to be able to make use of them—to guide them—there always stares us in the face that solitary question:

"Where—and how—did life start?"

* * * * *

We have seen in this volume a color photograph of corn as it grew four thousand years, perhaps, before the days of Adam and Eve.

It took less than eight seasons to carry this plant backward those ten thousand years.

How this plant was first taken back to the stage in which it was found by the American Indians, thus revealing the methods which they crudely used to improve it—and how it was taken back and back and back beyond the Pharaohs and then back forty centuries before the time of man— how we know these things to be true—and how, as a result of these experiments we are about to see it carried forward by several centuries—all of these things are reserved for a later chapter where

several direct color photograph prints bearing on
the evolution of corn. The
plant shown here is still
another variation, grown
only for ornamental pur-
poses, which Mr. Burbank
has brought about. As can
be seen from the print, the
leaves take on the brilliant
colors of the spectrum—
bright reds, yellows and
purples intermingling with
the green. For decorative
purposes rainbow corn
is quite a success.

space will permit the treatment which the subject deserves.

The illustration is cited here merely as one of thousands, typical of plant improvement, in which, in order to work forward a little, we must work backward ages and ages.

It is cited here to show that what is merely an interesting theory to the mass of the world's workers, becomes a definite, practical, working necessity to the man or woman who becomes interested in plant improvement.

It is cited here so that we may be helped to get a clearer mind picture of Mr. Burbank's viewpoint —of that viewpoint which, after all, has enabled him to become a leader in a new line, the founder of a new art—instead of remaining a nurseryman or gardener.

*   *   *   *   *

"In my viewpoint," says Mr. Burbank, "there is little that is new — little that has not been discovered by others — little that has not been accepted by scientists generally—little that requires explanation to those who simply see the same things that I have seen.

"I have no new theory of evolution to offer— perhaps only a few details to add to the theories which have already been worked out by men of science.

[284]

A BACKWARD GLANCE

"And I make these observations and conclusions of mine a part of this work for two reasons:

"First, because they are products not of imagination, reasoning, or any mental process—but the practical observations and conclusions which have gained force and proof, year by year, in a lifetime of experience with plants—throughout forty years of continuous devotion to the subject, during which time I have tried more than one hundred thousand separate experiments on plant life; and, as such, represent an important phase of my work.

"Second, because an ever-present interest in evolution—an ever-eager mind to peer backward and forward—is essential not only to the practice of plant improvement, but even to the barest understanding of it."

* * * * *

To gain the first quick glimpse, let us liken the process of evolution to a moving picture as it is thrown on the screen.

Imagine for example that some all-seeing camera had made a snapshot of Nature's progress each hundred years from the time when plant life started in our world to the present day.

Imagine that these progressive snapshots were joined together in a motion picture reel, and thrown in quick succession upon a screen.

We should see, no doubt, as the picture began to move, a tiny living being, a simple cell, the chemical product, perhaps, of salty water—so small that 900 of them would have to be assembled together to make a speck big enough for our human eyes to see.

As snapshot succeeded snapshot we should see that two of these microscopic simple cells in some way or other formed a partnership— possibly finding it easier to fight the elements of destruction in alliance than alone.

We should see, beyond doubt, that these partnerships joined other partnerships, and as partnership joined partnership, and group joined group, these amalgamations began to have an object beyond mere defense—that they began to organize for their own improvement, comfort, well being, or whatever was their guiding object.

We should see that, whereas each simple cell had within it all of the powers necessary to move about and live its life in its own crude way, yet with the amalgamation of the cells there came organization, development, improvement.

Some of the cells in each amalgamation, let us say, specialized on seeing, some on locomotion, some on digestion.

Thus, while each simple cell had all of these powers in a limited way, yet the new creature, as a result of specialization, could see better, move more readily, digest more easily, than the separate elements which went into it.

And so, through the early pictures of our reel, there would be spread before us the development of the little simple cell into more and more complex forms of life—first vegetable, then animal —into everything, finally, that lives and grows about us today—into us, ourselves.

* * * * *

In an actual motion picture as it is thrown on the screen, it is only the quick progressive succession of the pictures that makes us realize the sense of motion.

If we were to detach and examine a single film from the reel, it would show no movement. It would be as stationary and as fixed as a child's first kodak snapshot.

In the motion picture of Nature's evolution, the world, as we see it about us in our lifetime, represents but a single snapshot, detached from those which have preceded it and from those which are to succeed it.

And so, some of us—too many of us—not confronted with the same necessity which irresistibly leads the plant student into the study of these forces—viewing only the single, apparently unmoving picture before us, have concluded that there is no forward motion—that there has been no evolution—that there will be none.

The plant student, above all others, has the greatest facilities at his hand for observing not only the details of the picture which is now on the screen—but for gaining glimpses—fragmentary glimpses—of pictures which have preceded—of piecing these together—and of realizing that all that we have and are and will be must be a part of this slow, sure, forward-moving change that unfailingly traces itself back to the little simple salt-water cell.

As we go further and further into the work we shall begin to see the film fragments which to workers in other lines are obscured, unnoticed, unknown.

We shall be able to observe details of the process—carried home to us with undeniable conviction—indisputable to any man who believes what he actually sees — which will give us a realistic view of the whole motion picture which to the world at large has always been denied.

We shall find that, dealing, thus, with Nature's forces at first hand, our work will inspire an interest beyond even the interest of creating new forms of life.

And, as our work unfolds, the side lights which we shall see will clear up many or most of the doubts which are likely to take possession of us at the outset.

* * * * *

It may be well, at this point, however, to take space to refer to the single question most frequently asked by thousands of intelligent men and women who have visited Mr. Burbank's experiment farms.

This question, differing in form, as the individualities of the questioners differ, usually runs like this:

"If we are descendants of monkeys, why are not the monkeys turning into men today?"

* * * * *

Let us learn Mr. Burbank's answer to this question by turning to the golden-yellow California poppy, so called, and the three entirely new poppies (illustrated here in natural colors), which he produced from it.

In order to make clear the truth which the poppies prove, it is necessary to explain the successive steps of the operation.

Mr. Burbank first grew a yardful of the wild, golden-yellow poppies, such as cover California's hills.

The individual poppies of this yardful—a million of them, at a guess—resembled each other as closely as one rose resembles another rose on the same bush, or as one grape resembles another on the same bunch, as one pea resembles another in the same pod.

Yet among those million poppies—all looking alike to the unpracticed eye—there could be found by a close observer as many individual differences as could be found among any million human beings in the world.

Among those million poppies, each with its distinct individuality, Mr. Burbank found three which had a decided tendency to break away from the California poppy family and start a separate race of their own.

This same tendency could be observed among a million men, a million roses, a million peas, a million quartz crystals, or a million of any of Nature's creations.

Those one, or two, or three out of every million with tendencies to break away are sometimes called the freaks or "sports" of the species.

It seems as though Nature, never quite satisfied with her creations, is always experimenting, with the hope of creating a better result—yet limiting those experiments to such a small percentage that the mass of the race remains unchanged—its characteristics preserved—its general tendencies unaffected.

The California poppy, as it grows wild, is a rich

California Poppy

This direct color photograph print shows the wild
California poppy, so called, golden-yellow, as it grows in one
of Mr. Burbank's cactus patches. This common wild flower covers
California's hills at certain seasons and from it the State is
supposed to have received its name, "The Land of Fire."

The Golden Poppy Turned Crimson

*The first transformation which Mr. Burbank wrought in the
California poppy as explained in the text matter was to turn it to
crimson. The success of this experiment can be judged
from the color photograph print shown here.*

The California Poppy Turned White

*The next experiment which Mr. Burbank tried was to
eliminate the yellow of the wild poppy and produce, instead,
a white flower. The tips of the petals of this poppy are now pure
white, while the centers remain a very light cream-yellow, the
only suggestion of the bright golden yellow of its ancestors.*

The Poppy Turned Fire-Flame

*In his poppy variations Mr. Burbank found some
which, instead of blending the inherited characteristics showed
both distinctly in the same flower—lemon yellow edges with golden
yellow centers. These, perhaps the most beautiful result of his
experiment, he christened "The Fire-Flame Poppy."*

golden-yellow. In spite of individual differences, this color is the characteristic of the kind. It is a fixed characteristic, dating back at least to the time when California, because of the poppy covered hills, received its name—the land of fire— from the early Spanish navigators that ventured up and down the coast.

Out of the billion billions of wild poppies that have grown, each million has no doubt contained its freaks or its "sports"—its few experimental individuals which Nature has given the tendency to break away from the characteristics of their fellows.

Yet in the history of the California poppy family, as far back as we can trace, none of these freaks or "sports" had ever achieved its object.

Among the "sports" which Mr. Burbank found in the million poppies he grew were one with a crimson tendency, one with a white tendency, and one with a lemon-yellow, fiery-red tendency.

If Mr. Burbank had not intervened, these freaks, quite likely, would have perished without offspring.

But by nurturing them, separating them and saving their seeds, within a few brief seasons he was able to produce three new kinds of the California poppy.

Each kind had all of the parent poppy charac-

teristics but one. They were California poppies
in habits, in growth, in shape, in size, in form, in
grace, in texture, in beauty.

Yet in color they differed from the California
wild poppy almost as a violet differs from a daisy.

One of these freaks developed into the solid
crimson poppy, another into the pure white poppy,
and still another into the fire-flame poppy—all
shown here.

The details of method employed and the
application of these methods and the underlying
principles to the improvement of other flowers,
fruits, trees and useful and ornamental plants, will
be left for later chapters. But as an illustration,
this poppy experiment brings home three things:

First, that Nature creates no duplicates.

Second, that although each of Nature's creations has its own distinctive individuality, all the
time she takes special precautions to fix, preserve,
and make permanent the characteristics of each
of her races or kinds.

Third, that there is always present in all of
her creations the experimental tendency to break
away from fixed characteristics—to start new
races—to branch out into entirely new forms of
development. Through Mr. Burbank's intervention, in the case of the poppy, this tendency was
crowned with success; in ten thousand years,

Variations in Size

The poppy blossoms pictured in this direct color photograph print were picked out of a single ten foot bed and illustrate the variations in the size of seedlings as an aid to selection.

perhaps, without intervention at all, the same result might have been attained.

From the fern at the water's edge, to the apple tree which bears us luscious fruit—from the oyster that lies helpless in the bottom of Long Island Sound, to the human being who rakes it up, and eats it—every different form of life about us may, thus, be traced to the experiments which Nature is continually trying, in order to improve her creations.

As to the question so often asked, monkeys are no more turning into men than golden-yellow poppies are turning into crimson, white or fire-flame poppies.

In monkeys, as in men and poppies—and quartz crystals—there is ever present the tendency to break away from the kind, yet Nature is always alert to prevent the break—unless it demonstrates itself to be an advance, an improvement—from occurring.

She gives us, all of us, and everything—individuality, personality—unfailingly, always—at the same time preserving in each the general characteristics of its kind.

Yet all the time she is creating her freaks and "sports"—all the time she is trying new experiments—most of them doomed to die unproductive—with the hope that the thousand freaks

Another Color Variation

Unlike the fire-flame poppy in which the center is of one color and the outside edges of another, this poppy, unnamed, has vertical divisions on each petal, half crimson and half yellow. This is but one of the countless variations secured in the poppy experiment.

among a billion creations may show the way
toward a single improvement in a race.

*　*　*　*　*

In this hurried backward glance, we have, by
no means, gone back to the beginning of things.
Even the moving picture of Nature's course from
the salt-water cell to us, covering what seems an
infinity of time, may be but a single stationary
film in a still greater moving picture—and that,
too, but a part of a greater whole.

Indeed, the further we go into our subject, the
more we are convinced that instead of having
followed the thread of life to its beginning, we
have merely been following a raveling which leads
into one of its tiny strands.

The more we learn definitely about the process
which we trace back to the simple salt-water cell,
the more we are led to inquire into those other
forms of energy—into the chemical reactions—
into the vibrations which manifest themselves to
us as sound, heat, light—into electricity and those
manifestations whose discovery is more recent,
and whose nature is less well understood.

The more we observe the phenomena in our
own fields of activity, the more we realize the
futility of trying, in a single lifetime, to explore
Infinity.

The more content we feel, instead, to learn as

A Bouquet of Poppy Variations

It would be impossible, in a single photograph to show all of the variations which a single season's work brings forth. The bouquet shown here, however, when compared with the original golden-yellow parent, indicates the range of difference secured.

much as we can that is useful and practical, of the single strand of life's thread which has to do more immediately with the thing in hand.

* * * * *

"What do you put in the soil to make your canna lilies so big?"

"How often do you take up the bulbs of your gladioli?"

"How late do you keep your strawberry plants under glass?"

These, and a hundred others of their kind, are the questions which visitors at the experiment farm are continually asking Mr. Burbank.

It is not that Mr. Burbank undervalues the care of plants, or does not appreciate the importance of cultivation.

But his questioners fail to realize that his work has been with the *insides* of plants and not with their *externals*.

Of the details of working method—of the little tricks that save time—of Luther Burbank's bold innovations which many gardeners may have dreamed, but none have ever dared to do—of these, in the volumes to come, we shall find plenty.

Yet, we shall find ourselves, too, searching the times when things were not as they are, in order to get glimpses of things as they are to be—and all, not from the standpoint of theory, b·˙   ˙˙ to

The poppy still re-
tains many of its wild
characteristics, particularly
the production of great
quantities of seed. Seed
from Mr. Burbank's ex-
periment has been blown
over the grounds so that
poppies are likely to
spring up at any point.
In this direct color photograph print the golden-
below California poppy
and its new crimson
cousin are seen
growing wild
side by side.

help us in the very practical, useful work of coaxing from Nature new forms of plant life— better forms than, uncoaxed, she would give us— plants which because of their greater productivity will help us lower our constantly increasing cost of living—plants which will yield us entirely new substances to be used in manufactures— plants which will grow on what now are waste lands—plants which, by their better fruit, or their increased beauty, or their doubled yield, or their improved quality, will add to our individual pleasures and profits, and to the pleasures and profits of the whole world.

[END OF VOLUME I]

—In order to work forward a little, we must work backward ages and ages.

LIST OF
DIRECT COLOR PHOTOGRAPH PRINTS
IN VOLUME I

ANNEX

CPSIA information can be obtained
at www.ICGtesting.com
Printed in the USA
LVHW081501190421
684905LV00002B/90